T0329025

ABOUT
EDWIN DROOD

ABOUT
EDWIN DROOD

Cambridge
at the University Press
1911

CAMBRIDGE
UNIVERSITY PRESS

32 Avenue of the Americas, New York NY 10013-2473, USA

Cambridge University Press is part of the University of Cambridge.

It furthers the University's mission by disseminating knowledge in the pursuit of
education, learning and research at the highest international levels of excellence.

www.cambridge.org
Information on this title: www.cambridge.org/9781107458871

© Cambridge University Press 1911

First published 1911
First paperback edition 2014

A catalogue record for this publication is available from the British Library

ISBN 978-1-107-45887-1 Paperback

To the members of the "Cloisterham Syndicate," and to our kind guide, Mr Edwin Harris, I dedicate these Notes and Queries, in memory of our exploration of Dickensland, 3—6 July 1909.

H. J.

Trinity College, Cambridge.
17 *July* 1910.

PREFACE

THESE pages do not pretend to fill by conjecture the gaps in Charles Dickens' unfinished story. It is certain that he had bestowed especial pains upon the structure of his plot, and that he was anxious to keep his secret till the right moment came for its disclosure. This being so, I do not believe that any ingenuity of conjecture can supply what Dickens did not live to write. But the fragment which we possess has always seemed to me a masterpiece: and, thus thinking, I attempt, not to add to what Dickens has left to us, but to make clear and definite so much of the story as is covered by the twenty-three extant chapters, and to elucidate certain details which seem to me to have been misunderstood or overlooked. I am moved to do this by the publication of Mr J. Cuming Walters' *Clues to Dickens's "Mystery of Edwin Drood"* and Mr Andrew Lang's *Puzzle of Dickens's Last Plot*, works which, inasmuch as they deal comprehensively and minutely with the extant fragment, invite criticism and assist reconstruction. To both I am deeply indebted; for, whatever may be thought of Mr Cuming Walters' theory that Datchery is Helena disguised, his presentment of it has been a help and a stimulus to all of us: and, while I demur to Mr Lang's identification of Datchery with Edwin Drood, I am always, I hope, mindful of his timely warning that the novelist is apt to be the slave of his story. If in the course of my argument I have to say more about matters in which I differ from these scholars than about matters in which I agree with them, I hope that they will not think me ungrateful. On the contrary, I never forget how, at a time when I was an invalid and solitary, their speculations occupied my thoughts and gave me food for meditation.

But, besides these comprehensive reviews, there are in the *Dickensian*, *The Cambridge Review*, and other periodicals, a host of papers and notes. I do not attempt a bibliography; but I have endeavoured to give such references as are likely to be helpful.

In citing *Edwin Drood* I have given the pages of the "Fireside Dickens." For the convenience of those who use the original edition or the "Popular Edition," I have shown in tabular form the pagination of the chapters in the three editions. To the publishers, Messrs Chapman and Hall, I am indebted for permission to make quotations and to reproduce the cover of the monthly parts.

I am grateful to many friends for valuable criticisms and suggestions: and, in particular, to Dr Bonney, who kindly wrote out for me his own theories; to the Provost of King's, who told me of the existence of the manuscript at the Victoria and Albert Museum; to Mr H. H. Brindley, who enlightened my ignorance about the operation of opium; to Mr A. E. Shipley, who organised an expedition to Rochester, which did much to help me to visualise Cloisterham; and to Mr Edwin Harris of Rochester, who seems to me to know all that can be known about Dickens and Dickensland, and has freely given me the benefit of his erudition.

In conclusion, I thank the Syndics of the Cambridge University Press for undertaking the publication of this little book.

H. J.

17 *July* 1910.

My references are to the pages of the "Fireside Dickens," published by Messrs Chapman and Hall and Mr Henry Frowde. The following table equates the pagination of this edition with that of the original edition and with that of their "Popular" edition.

Chapters	Original	Popular	Fireside
i	1	7	11
ii	3	10	17
iii	12	21	28
iv	21	33	42
v	28	42	52
vi	33	49	59
vii	40	59	69
viii	47	68	80
ix	54	77	91
x	65	92	106
xi	75	106	120
xii	86	120	134
xiii	97	134	150
xiv	104	144	163
xv	114	158	177
xvi	121	166	188
xvii	129	176	198
xviii	140	191	213
xix	147	200	222
xx	153	207	232
xxi	161	217	244
xxii	165	223	250
xxiii	178	240	269

CONTENTS

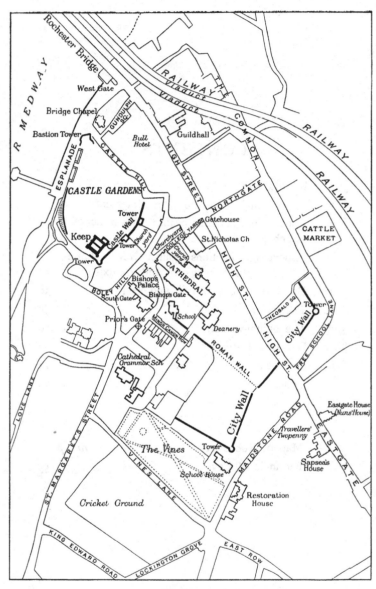

Rochester

Based upon the Ordnance Survey Map with the sanction of the
Controller of H.M. Stationery Office

§ i. *Introduction.*

It is well known that Dickens was scrupulously reticent about the plot of his last story, and that he left behind him no notes for the chapters which he did not live to write. Nevertheless there is one all-important tradition which must not be neglected. Mr John Forster, in his *Life of Charles Dickens*, iii 425, 426, has a very precise account of the plot which Dickens had proposed to himself in *Edwin Drood.* " The story, I learnt immediately afterward, was to be that of the murder of a nephew by his uncle; the originality of which was to consist in the review of the murderer's career by himself at the close, when its temptations were to be dwelt upon as if, not he the culprit, but some other man, were the tempted. The last chapters were to be written in the condemned cell, to which his wickedness, all elaborately elicited from him as if told of another, had brought him. Discovery by the murderer of the utter uselessness of the murder for its object, was to follow hard upon commission of the deed ; but all discovery of the murderer was to be baffled till towards the close, when, by means of a gold ring which has resisted the corrosive effects of the lime into which he had thrown the body, not only the person murdered was to be identified but the locality of the crime and the man who committed it. So much was told to me before any of the book was written; and it will be recollected that the ring, taken by Drood to be given to his betrothed only if their engagement went on, was brought away with him from their last interview. Rosa was to marry Tartar, and Crisparkle the sister of Landless, who was himself, I think, to have perished in assisting Tartar finally to unmask and seize the murderer."

The extant fragment, so far as it goes, is perfectly consistent with the scheme here described. Directly or indirectly we hear that Jasper leads a double life; that, despite his real or pretended affection for his nephew, under the influence of opium he "threatens" him; that, not under the influence of opium, he provokes a quarrel between Drood and Landless, and subsequently makes the most of it; that he undertakes an "unaccountable expedition" with Durdles; and that, at a later visit to the opium den, he babbles about the accomplishment of a long contemplated design. The discovery that the engagement of Edwin and Rosa is at an end follows soon after the disappearance. That the old betrothal ring, which, though Jasper did not know it, Edwin had in his possession, and, when he parted from Rosa, still retained, was hereafter to play an important part in the dénoûment, we are warned in an emphatic aside: "there was one chain forged in the moment of that small conclusion" [i.e. Edwin's determination to say nothing to Rosa about the ring], "riveted to the foundations of heaven and earth, and gifted with invincible force to hold and drag." Thus far, the story left half-told is in exact accord with the forecast. But, whereas, according to Forster, (1) Drood's disappearance was to remain unexplained until the betrothal ring should discover the murderer, the victim, and the locality of the crime, and (2) the murderer was to write his confessions in the condemned cell, the extant fragment stops short of these things. It is indeed possible, and even probable, that Grewgious has anxiously asked himself what had become of the ring : but there is nothing to guide him in the search for it ; and accordingly, within the limits of the fragment the disappearance of Edwin Drood is still a "mystery." It is a "mystery" for us who know, not only what is common knowledge to the inhabitants of Cloisterham, but also the observations of the opium-woman, and the suspicions of Grewgious and Rosa : and it is all the more a "mystery" for those who have not our advantages; for the inhabitants of Cloisterham, for the opium-woman, and for Grewgious and Rosa and their allies.

To some critics however, and notably to Mr Proctor and Mr Lang, the plot described by Forster seems too simple and obvious: and accordingly they suppose that, though Jasper had planned the murder and believed himself to have committed it, Drood escaped, and within the limits of the fragment is already occupied in tracking his assailant.

Now it is certain that Dickens intended to keep his readers in doubt about Drood's fate. For in a

tentative list of possible titles for the book the last
three are " The disappearance of Edwin Drood," "The
mystery of Edwin Drood," " Dead ? or Alive ? "
This being so, both theories, the theory countenanced
by Forster, that Jasper accomplished the murder of
Drood, and the theory of Mr Proctor and Mr Lang,
that Drood escaped, are admissible : and I propose in
due course to take both into consideration.

§ ii. *The chronology of the extant fragment.*

In the first place it is worth while to study the chronology of the twenty-three chapters which Dickens completed.

Chapters i to iii cover two days when the year was waning, p. 17. In ch. i Jasper, who has entered the opium-den at midnight, p. 12, leaves it on the morning of the first of these two days, and returns to Cloisterham in time for vespers, p. 16. In ch. ii, later in this same day—which is a Wednesday, p. 20, and Rosa's birthday, p. 21—he welcomes Edwin Drood. In ch. iii, the next day, Thursday, pp. 31 and 33, Edwin and Rosa take a walk together which is not a happy one.

Chapters iv and v describe the events of a single evening later in the year. In ch. iv Jasper takes wine and sups with Sapsea, commends the inscription to be placed on the Sapsea monument[1], and makes acquaintance with Durdles. In ch. v Jasper quarrels with Deputy.

Chapters vi to ix relate events which took place not

[1] Mr Proctor and Mr Walters suppose that the Sapsea vault was in the crypt: see *Watched by the Dead*, p. 74, and *Clues*, pp. 24, 109. This is an oversight. That the Sapsea monument was in the burial-ground adjoining the cathedral is proved by pp. 53 and 219, 220; and Durdles' talk about the key at pp. 49, 50 precludes the conjecture that the vault and the monument were distinct.

very long before Christmas ; say, early in December :
for in ch. xi, p. 125, not long before Christmas,
Grewgious speaks of his visit described in ch. ix as
having been made "lately." These chapters, vi to ix,
cover a Thursday and the Monday and Tuesday next
ensuing. That is to say, ch. vi tells us, how one
morning Crisparkle and his mother read a letter written
by Honeythunder from London on Wednesday, p. 61,
in which he announces the arrival of Neville and Helena
Landless for the following Monday, and how on the
appointed day Honeythunder unexpectedly accom-
panied his wards and spoilt Mrs Crisparkle's dinner
party : ch. vii records Neville's talk with Crisparkle,
the scene in the drawing-room, and the confidences of
Helena and Rosa : ch. viii tells of the quarrel between
Neville and Edwin, which Jasper foments and afterwards reports to Crisparkle : ch. ix recounts the events
of the following day, Tuesday ; namely, the chatter at
Miss Twinkleton's, and Mr Grewgious' visit to Rosa.
At pp. 101, 102—compare p. 80—we learn that Edwin,
who left Cloisterham that morning, would return at
Christmas ; and that Grewgious, who would entertain
Bazzard at dinner on Christmas Day, would come to
Cloisterham, presumably on Dec. 26, if Rosa "had
anything particular to say to him." At pp. 104, 105
Grewgious tells Jasper that at Christmas Edwin and
Rosa would complete their preparations for May, and
that, when they had done so, nothing would remain for
the guardians but to have everything ready for their
formal release from their trusts on Edwin's birthday.
Grewgious and Jasper part on good terms.

Between ch. ix and ch. x some days have elapsed. As appears in Crisparkle's conversations with his mother, with Neville and Helena, and with Jasper, Crisparkle has had time to study the two Landlesses; and on the strength of his observations he asks Jasper to intercede with Edwin. After "some close internal calculation" Jasper consents, and on the third day after this conversation he brings to Crisparkle a letter from Edwin proposing that the three should meet at dinner on Saturday, Dec. 24, and "shake hands all round there and then."

The interval between ch. x and ch. xi is not a long one: for, as has been said, in ch. xi, p. 125, Grewgious speaks of his visit to Cloisterham described in ch. ix as having been made "lately." Again the interval between ch. xi, Drood's visit to Grewgious, and ch. xii, "the unaccountable expedition," is not long: for Grewgious assumes, p. 124, that Drood will very soon go to Cloisterham for Christmas. "The unaccountable expedition" of ch. xii was on "the first day" of the week which ended with Christmas Eve, p. 142: that is to say, as clearly appears from a comparison of p. 142 with p. 166, on the first week-day of that week, namely, Monday the 19th. Now it is reasonable to suppose that Bazzard was not in attendance at Staple Inn on Saturday night. This being so, we may fairly assign ch. xi to Friday, Dec. 16. It is however conceivable that Drood's visit to Grewgious in ch. xi was contemporaneous with "the unaccountable expedition" of ch. xii on Monday, Dec. 19.

The chapters which follow, xii to xvi, describe in

detail the events of Dec. 19 to Dec. 28, and, in general terms, the subsequent situation. The dates of some of these chapters, but not of all, can be exactly determined. We have seen that "the unaccountable expedition" of ch. xii was on Monday the 19th. "The concluding ceremony" at Miss Twinkleton's in ch. xiii may have been on Tuesday the 20th, Wednesday the 21st, or Thursday the 22nd. The parting of Edwin and Rosa was on Friday the 23rd, p. 159. Edwin's intention is (pp. 159, 161) to stay till Monday, to see Grewgious when he arrives, and to leave Cloisterham before Grewgious speaks with Jasper : compare p. 196. Edwin says nothing to Rosa about the betrothal ring, which he will now restore to Grewgious[1].

In ch. xiv "When shall these three meet again?" we have the history of Saturday, Dec. 24. Neville prepares for his expedition, and talks with Crisparkle and with Helena. Edwin visits the jeweller, and has

---

[1] It is not the retention of the ring, but Edwin's silence about it, which Dickens emphasises: "there was one chain forged in the moment of that small conclusion, riveted to the foundations of heaven and earth, and gifted with invincible force to hold and drag." I understand Dickens to imply that, if Edwin had told Rosa about the ring, his possession of it would have become common knowledge, and Jasper would have been on his guard : but that so long as Grewgious alone was aware of its existence, he was master of the situation. If, later, Grewgious, presumably through Durdles, heard of its discovery, an advertisement for a ring, known to have been in the possession of the late Edwin Drood, would draw the murderer to the place where the body was made away with. It will be observed that, if, as some have supposed, Drood escaped and immediately communicated with Grewgious, the ring ceases to be of any importance as a proof of identity.

a remarkable conversation with the opium-woman. Jasper, who has spent the previous night in the opiumden, shops, visits Sapsea, and talks with Crisparkle. The three, Jasper, Drood, and Landless, meet at dinner at the gatehouse. There is a great storm. Edwin and Neville go to the river. The next morning, Sunday, Dec. 25, Jasper announces Edwin's disappearance.

In ch. xv Neville, who has started for his walk early on the morning of Sunday, Dec. 25, is pursued and brought back to Cloisterham. The search for Edwin is carried on throughout Sunday the 25th, Monday the 26th, and Tuesday the 27th. On the evening of Tuesday the 27th, Jasper on his return to the gatehouse is visited by Grewgious[1], who has seen Rosa

---

[1] Mr Lang, *Puzzle*, pp. 59, 60, supposes that Grewgious arrived at Cloisterham on Saturday, December 24, and visited the churchyard that he might "'consecrate a night of memories and sighs' to his lost lady love," Mrs Bud, who, "we have been told, was buried hard by the Sapsea monument." Now we know that the late Mr Drood was buried in that neighbourhood, p. 53: but I do not remember that there is any such statement about the burial place of Rosa's mother. However this may be, it is certain that Grewgious did not come to Cloisterham before Monday the 26th. For, in the absence of a summons from Rosa, he was to entertain Bazzard at dinner on Christmas Day, p. 102: and, although Rosa has sent for her guardian, it follows from her conversation with Edwin, p. 159, that she has not asked him to cancel his engagement to Bazzard: if Grewgious had come to Cloisterham on the Saturday, his presence might have created serious difficulties. Moreover, Rosa's statement at p. 196 that "Edwin disappeared before Mr Grewgious appeared," is conclusive evidence that Grewgious did not arrive on Christmas Eve.

and Helena. Grewgious tells Jasper of the parting of
Edwin and Rosa, and Jasper has a fit or swoon.

In ch. xvi—still the evening of Tuesday the 27th
—Jasper recovers his senses, and talks, first with
Grewgious, afterwards with Grewgious and Crisparkle.
In his talk with Grewgious Jasper expresses his conviction that Drood has absconded in order to avoid
awkward explanations; and, when Crisparkle comes in,
he affirms that Grewgious' communication "has hope-
fully influenced" his "mind, in spite of its having been…
profoundly impressed against young Landless." Now it
is plain to the reader that Grewgious, though he "does
not know what to think" and "cannot make up his
mind," has completely changed his attitude to Jasper,
and "has suspicions" of the gravest sort in regard to
him; compare p. 270. But he says nothing about
them: and Crisparkle, impressed by Jasper's apparent
candour, tells his companions of Neville's second out-
break of temper and of his jealousy. On leaving the
gatehouse Crisparkle walks aimlessly to the weir. The
next morning, Wednesday the 28th, he returns thither,
and finds Edwin's watch and shirt-pin. Neville is
"detained and redetained," but no further evidence
is forthcoming. Presently he leaves Cloisterham. On
the strength of the discovery of the watch and the
shirt-pin, Jasper declares himself convinced that Drood
has been murdered, and devotes himself to the destruction of the murderer.

It would seem then that, if these chapters follow
one another in chronological order,—and there is no
reason why they should not do so,—their dates are as

follows : xii, Dec. 19 ; the beginning of xiii, Dec. 20, 21, or 22 ; the end of xiii, Dec. 23 ; xiv, Dec. 24 ; xv, Dec. 25, 26, 27 ; xvi, Dec. 27, 28, and following days.

And now there is a break in the narrative. When it is resumed at ch. xvii, we are told that "full half a year had come and gone." The incidents recorded in ch. xvii and in chs. xix to xxii follow closely upon one another, and do not occupy more than six or seven days. There is indeed an interval between ch. xvii and ch. xix : but it is a very short one. For (1) in ch. xxi, p. 244, when Crisparkle arrives, Grewgious remarks that " it was particularly kind of him to come, for he had but just gone," where Grewgious plainly refers to Crisparkle's visit described in ch. xvii : and (2) at p. 247, Tartar speaks of having made acquaintance with Neville "only within a day or so"; compare ch. xvii, pp. 209–212. Further, we know from Crisparkle, ch. xvii, p. 206, that Helena is to join Neville in London, for a long visit, "next week." If then we are to bring ch. xvii into close connection with ch. xix, and at the same time to provide that Helena's arrival may fall in the following week, we must suppose that Crisparkle and Tartar visited Neville on a Friday or a Saturday, and that Helena came to London on the following Monday. Now, if Dec. 25 of the previous year was a Sunday, and the current year was not leap-year, July 2 was a Sunday. In the following scheme I take this day as my basis.

Ch. xvii. Friday, June 30. Crisparkle comes to London; sees Honeythunder, Grewgious, and Neville;

and returns to Cloisterham. Tartar makes acquaintance with Neville.

Ch. xix. Miss Twinkleton's school having broken up on Saturday, July 1, on the following Monday, July 3, Helena comes to London to join her brother. In the afternoon Jasper visits Rosa and frightens her with his wild talk.

Ch. xx. The same day. Rosa flies to London. Grewgious establishes her at the hotel in Furnival's.

Ch. xxi. Tuesday, July 4. Crisparkle arrives. Tartar introduces himself to Crisparkle, Grewgious, and Rosa.

Ch. xxii. The same day. Rosa explains the situation to Helena, p. 252. Helena raises the question "whether it would be best to wait until any more maligning and pursuing of Neville on the part of this wretch shall disclose itself, or to try to anticipate it." Crisparkle refers the question to Grewgious, who holds that "if you could steal a march upon a brigand or a wild beast, you had better do it," and that "John Jasper was a brigand and a wild beast in combination." Crisparkle goes home. Grewgious engages lodgings for Rosa. Tartar takes Rosa and Grewgious up the river.

On the next day but one, p. 260, Thursday, July 6, Miss Twinkleton joins Rosa, and then "the days crept on."

Thus the sequence of chapters xvii and xix to xxii is perfect.

I come now to ch. xviii, which, so far, I have ignored. "At about this time" Datchery appears at

Cloisterham, goes to the Crozier, engages lodgings at Tope's, makes acquaintance with Sapsea, Jasper, Durdles, and Deputy. The position of this chapter between ch. xvii and ch. xix, with the opening words "At about this time," suggests that Datchery made his appearance at Cloisterham on or about June 30 or July 1, and before the events recorded in ch. xix. But there is no obvious connection between Datchery's doings in ch. xviii and the consecutive narrative contained in chapters xvii and xix to xxii.

Again there is nothing to show what length of time has elapsed between ch. xviii and ch. xxiii. In ch. xxiii Jasper goes to a hotel near Aldersgate Street, and thence to the opium-den, where the old woman draws from him the story of his "journey." When Jasper leaves, the old woman waits for him, tracks him home, and learns his name from Datchery, who gives her money. She tells him of her talk with Edwin. Datchery questions Deputy about her, and tells him to find out where she lives. The next morning at the Cathedral she betrays to Datchery and to Deputy her animosity against Jasper. And so the fragment ends.

This chronological statement may be thought tedious and pedantic. But it suggests that, so far as the narrative goes in the twenty-three chapters, Dickens has studiously thought out the connection of the several incidents included in it, and has not, like Scott in *Rob Roy*, left chronology to take care of itself. There is however one incident, the appearance of Datchery at Cloisterham, which does not, like the rest, fall easily and immediately into its place in the sequence of events. As has been seen, Datchery appears to have gone to the Crozier on or about June 30 or July 1: and, for anything we know thus far, he may have done so. But, at present, we have not been able to connect his arrival with any of the particular events recorded in chapters xvii and xix to xxii. I shall return to this matter later.

§ iii. *Jasper's machinations against Edwin Drood: chapters i–xiv.*

Very many readers of *The Mystery*, and amongst them Mr Proctor and Mr Lang, hold that Edwin Drood escaped with his life : but all or nearly all, Mr Proctor and Mr Lang not excepted, acknowledge that Jasper tried to murder his nephew and believed himself to have succeeded. This being so, I may defer what I have to say about Edwin's fate, and proceed at once to inquire—(1) Where and how did Jasper murder Drood, or attempt to murder him? (2) Where and how did Jasper dispose of Drood's body, or attempt to dispose of it?

I propose then at this point to review the several passages which may be thought to bear upon these questions, adding in each case a few sentences of comment.

(1) In ch. iv, meeting Durdles by appointment at Sapsea's house, Jasper has an opportunity of examining the key of Mr Sapsea's monument and clinking it against the keys of two other monuments, p. 50. Durdles bids him "take care of the wards," and warns him that he "can't make a pitch pipe of 'em." In

ch. v, later in the same evening, Jasper, on his way from Sapsea's to the gatehouse, finds Deputy stoning Durdles in the neighbourhood of the Cathedral, and retracing his steps, brings Durdles to his "house, or hole in the city wall," p. 140, near Sapsea's end of High Street. As they go, in reply to a direct question from Jasper, p. 55, Durdles tells him how, by tapping with his hammer, he is able to discover the contents of vaults and of the coffins within them.

Mr Proctor suggests, *Watched by the Dead*, p. 42, and Mr Lang agrees with him, *Puzzle*, p. 9, that Jasper's purpose in clinking the keys together is to learn how to distinguish by the sound Sapsea's key, and hence it has been inferred that on the fatal night Jasper deposited Drood's body in the Sapsea monument. But Durdles' "dogged" explanation, p. 50, "When Durdles puts a touch or a finish upon his work, no matter where, inside or outside, Durdles likes to look at his work all round, and see that his work is a-doing him credit," and his account of his "gift," p. 56, must surely convince Jasper that any receptacle which Durdles could tap with his hammer would be an unsatisfactory hiding-place, and that the Sapsea monument would be exceptionally so. Hence, though with Mr Proctor and Mr Lang I suppose that Jasper had thought of depositing the body of his victim in the Sapsea monument, I am confident that, for excellent reasons, he now abandons this first scheme.

(2) The arrival of Neville Landless suggests a second expedient. In ch. viii "Daggers Drawn," Jasper tries to stir up a quarrel between Edwin and

Neville, and very nearly succeeds. But at p. 117, after "close internal calculation," Jasper undertakes to arrange a friendly meeting for Christmas Eve with a view to a reconciliation.

That is to say, Jasper had next thought to use Neville as his catspaw for the destruction of Edwin. But Crisparkle's influence with Neville is strong, and Neville himself, though passionate, is generous. So Jasper's plot must be again modified: and when, on the night of "the unaccountable expedition," p. 141, listening to snatches of Crisparkle's talk with Neville, he "watches Neville as though his eye were at the trigger of a loaded rifle," and presently "bursts into a fit of laughter," we have indications of a change in his plan of campaign. Presumably his third thought is to make away with Edwin in such a manner that Neville, his new rival, will be suspected of the crime.

(3) At the beginning of ch. xxiii, Jasper, replying under the influence of opium to the skilful interrogatory of the opium-woman, who now knows "how to make him talk," p. 276, tells her that over and over again in her den he has done something which he had in his mind but had not quite determined to do; that this something was "a hazardous and perilous journey over abysses where a slip would be destruction"; that there was a fellow-traveller whose presence was indispensable; that the journey was always made in fancy "in the same way," "in the way in which it was really made at last"; but that, when it came to be made finally, there was "no struggle, no consciousness of peril, no entreaty,—and yet I never saw *that* before." "Look at

it! look what a poor, mean, miserable thing it is! *That* must be real!": and seemingly we may connect with these sentences, p. 276, the previous sentence, p. 274, "Look down, look down! you see what lies at the bottom there?" We are not told in ch. xxiii what the scene of the journey was: but we may be quite sure that it was the tower of Cloisterham Cathedral. For, Jasper's words in ch. xxiii "The dawn again," "I always made the journey first, before the changes of colours and the great landscapes and glittering processions began," echo the first paragraph of ch. i "The dawn," and in the first sentence of that first paragraph Jasper sees "an ancient English Cathedral Tower" strangely dominating his dreams.

Now when Jasper, while he connects what he had in his mind with the doing of it in fancy, distinguishes between the doing of it in fancy and the real doing of it, it is quite clear that the real doing of it is no mere imagination. Furthermore, the opium-woman assumes that his babbling is significant; and we know from her conversation with Edwin on Christmas Eve that she had already elicited certain important facts, though, for want of knowledge of the persons concerned and their relations to one another, she had not fully understood Jasper's utterances. But, by admission, he is plotting the destruction of Drood. This being so, when we are told that Jasper had had in his mind the tower of the Cathedral, and a perilous journey over abysses with an indispensable fellow traveller, and that, when the journey was really made, there was "no struggle, no consciousness of peril, no entreaty," but that "a poor, mean, miserable thing," which was nevertheless "real," lay "down below at the bottom," I am constrained to believe that we have here Jasper's confession of the place and the manner of the crime. He had ascended the tower with Edwin, and he had seen Edwin's body lying down below, presumably at the foot of the staircase by which they had ascended.

And when I examine the speculations of Mr Proctor, Mr Lang, and Mr Walters, I am confirmed in this belief. Mr Proctor and Mr Lang suppose that Jasper partially strangled Drood near the Cathedral, and then deposited his body in the Sapsea monument, from which he was rescued, according to Mr Proctor, by Durdles, according to Mr Lang, with the help of Grewgious. Again, Mr Walters supposes, *Clues*, p. 33, that "Drood was to be encountered near the Cathedral, drugged, and then strangled with the black silk scarf that Jasper wore round his own neck." But if Edwin was to be strangled or partially strangled outside the Cathedral on level ground, "the perilous journey over abysses" which has occupied Jasper's thoughts and visions and at last has been realised in fact, ceases to be important, or relevant, or intelligible.

Accordingly Mr Walters, though he refers to "the journey" at pp. 28 and 90, makes no attempt to explain it, and even tells us, p. 90, that "the old woman had made him talk, but his talk was 'unintelligible.'" We have however a distinct assurance that this is not so. For, when Jasper has ceased to be talkative, the old woman, *Mystery*, p. 276, "croaks

under her breath "—"I heard ye say once, when I was
lying where you're lying, and you were making your
speculations upon me, ' Unintelligible!'   I heard you
say so, of two more than me.   But don't ye be too sure
always ; don't ye be too sure, beauty!...Not so potent
as it once was ? Ah!   Perhaps not at first.   You may
be more right there.   Practice makes perfect.   I may
have learnt the secret how to make ye talk, deary."

Similarly Mr Proctor makes short work with this
part of ch. xxiii.   "We learn afterwards," he says,
Watched by the Dead, p. 73, "when Jasper goes
through the scene again under the influence of opium,
that, though 'there was no struggle, no consciousness
of peril, no entreaty,' there was *something* which, in his
many visions of the event before it happened, he had
never seen.   'I never saw *that* before,' he says.   But
this need not necessarily relate to the struggle itself,
but to Jasper's thoughts of the struggle after he had
learned from Grewgious how idle had been his villainy."
That is to say, Mr Proctor ignores the talk about "a
hazardous and perilous journey over abysses " in company with a fellow traveller ; and, as he cannot connect
the words " I never saw *that* before" with the attack
upon Drood, assumes, but does not explain, a reference
to Jasper's subsequent thoughts about it.

Mr Lang however faces the question which Mr
Walters and Mr Proctor evade.   Recognising the
importance of Jasper's mutterings, and perceiving that
in his theory of Jasper's attempt upon Drood there is
no room for "the journey over abysses," Mr Lang asks,
Puzzle, p. 41, "Is part of Jasper's vision reminiscent—

the brief, unresisting death—while another part is a separate vision, is *prospective*, 'premonitory'? Does he see himself pitching Neville Landless off the tower top, or see him fallen from the Cathedral roof? Is Neville's body '*that*'—' I never saw *that* before. Look what a poor miserable mean thing it is! *That* must be real.' Jasper never saw *that*—the dead body below the height—before. *This* vision, I think, is of the future, not of the past, and is meant to bewilder the reader who thinks that the whole represents the slaying of Drood." That is to say, Mr Lang supposes that the single phrase "no struggle, no consciousness of peril, no entreaty" represents a vision reminiscent of the attempted murder of Drood; but that the words which are separated from that phrase by no more than a hyphen—"and yet I never saw *that* before," and the rest of two pages, 274–276, represent "a separate vision," prospective of the capture of Jasper and the death of Neville on the Christmas Eve which is still to come, *Puzzle*, pp. 72, 88. For myself, I cannot believe that Dickens, however much he may have wished "to bewilder the reader," has intruded into babblings which represent a prospective, prophetic, vision eight words which represent a vision reminiscent of the past: and I demur altogether to the theory that "the perilous journey over abysses" is a vision of the coming retribution. For (*a*) "the journey" was "something which Jasper had in his mind, but had not quite determined to do," he had "done it over and over again" in fancy, he had made the journey "always in the same way," "in the way in which it was really made at last." Surely

this is a clear statement that "the journey" belongs to
the past and not to the future; (*b*) what Jasper did
"was pleasant to do"; he came to the opium-den "on
purpose to take the journey, to get the relief, and he
got it." Plainly "the journey" is the crime which
Jasper hankered after: he could find neither pleasure
nor relief in the thought of the retribution which is
hereafter to come upon himself; (*c*) the echo of the
first paragraph of the story at p. 275—"Yes! I always
made the journey first, before the changes of colours
and the great landscapes and glittering processions
began"—shows that "the journey" which he was to
make with an indispensable fellow traveller, was in
Jasper's thoughts before he knew of Landless' existence.

In short, if Jasper flung or pushed Drood down
the staircase of the tower, the babblings of the opium-
den are, as the old woman plainly recognises, p. 276,
quite intelligible. On the other hand, if Drood was
attacked outside the Cathedral on level ground, the
babblings have no meaning whatever, and at best are
unjustifiable mystifications.

(4) In ch. xii, "A night with Durdles," Jasper repairs
to Durdles' "house, or hole in the city wall" near the
other end of High Street, and chances to hear from him
of the destructive powers of quicklime. Thence they
come by Minor Canon Corner to the Close, and enter the
Cathedral from the crypt, unlocking both the doors with
a key which belongs to Durdles. Next, opening an iron
gate with a key "confided to Jasper," presumably by
the Dean, compare p. 135, they ascend the tower by
its winding staircase and look down upon Cloisterham,

"fair to see in the moonlight." They descend. On the way down Durdles, who has emptied Jasper's bottle, "has stumbled twice, and cut an eyebrow open once": and in the crypt he sleeps long and heavily. Whilst he sleeps, Jasper takes from him the key of the crypt, but presently brings it back and lays it beside him. Jasper remarks upon the strength of "the good stuff," and Durdles is at times conscious that Jasper is closely scrutinizing him. Four times, pp. 140, 141, 146, 149, this expedition is described as "unaccountable": and at p. 149 it "comes to an end—for the time."

Surely this "unaccountable expedition," made with Durdles on Dec. 19, is a rehearsal of "the journey" which, as we have seen, Jasper proposes to make, and actually makes, with the indispensable fellow traveller: and presumably the study of the rehearsal will enable us to anticipate some details of the tragedy[1]. From the top of the tower Jasper "contemplates the scene, and especially that stillest part of it which the Cathedral overshadows." Presumably one of his purposes is to estimate the suitability of the Close for murder and concealment. But I think that the estimate formed is unfavourable. "But," we are told, "he contemplates Durdles quite as curiously, and Durdles is by times conscious of his watchful eyes," p. 146. Indeed, later, Durdles asks, "What do you suspect me of, Mister

[1] In Dickens' scanty "Plans" for this chapter he says—"lays the ground for the manner of the murder, to come out at last. Keep the boy suspended." I understand the last sentence to mean that Deputy is not here to be prominent, but that we are to be reminded of his existence: compare pp. 148, 149.

Jarsper? Let them as has any suspicions of Durdles name 'em." "I've no suspicions of you, my good Mr Durdles," says Jasper. I think that Jasper's reply is truthful. He had been anxious to know whether the "good stuff" was potent enough to serve its purpose ; and, whether Durdles has any suspicion of him and his designs. He is now satisfied both of the potency of the "good stuff" and of Durdles' innocence of any suspicion : Durdles is too drunk to be dangerous.

Meanwhile, as has been seen, when they descend into the crypt he "has stumbled twice, and cut an eyebrow open once." Durdles' disasters are suggestive. Arrived in the crypt, Durdles sleeps, but Jasper has more things than one to attend to. Plainly, he must make a wax impression of the key with which Durdles has opened the outside door of the crypt and the door between the crypt and the Cathedral: and accordingly we are given to understand that Jasper took the key from him while he slept and restored it before he awoke. Again, Jasper had to find a place in which the body of his victim might safely be bestowed. He has already perceived that the Sapsea monument, or indeed any other tomb accessible to Durdles' hammer, would be a very unsatisfactory hiding place. Moreover, he knows that, however lonely the Close may be, it would be difficult and dangerous to transport a corpse from place to place outside the Cathedral. Could he find a place of concealment within it? Now it is inconceivable that Durdles, whenever as "contractor for rough repairs" he wanted material for use

at the Cathedral, went to fetch it from his yard at the
other end of the town : he must have had ready to
hand, and therefore presumably in the crypt, wood,
stone, bricks, mortar, quicklime, and so forth. Indeed,
Mr Edwin Harris tells me that, when *Edwin Drood*
was written, the unpaved floor of the crypt was "littered
with fragments of monuments, heaps of rubbish, and
building materials."   Let us suppose then that Jasper,
as he walks to and fro "among the lanes of light,"
finds a mound of lime similar to that which Durdles in
his yard had described as "quick enough to eat your
boots : with a little handy stirring, quick enough to eat
your bones."   To make away with the body of the
victim would be better than to deposit it where it
might be found : Durdles' hammer could do nothing
against a heap of lime : and no casual passer-by could
watch what was done in the crypt.   The scheme is
now complete.   Drood, under the influence of strong
drink is to be flung or pushed down the winding staircase of the tower, and his body is to be deposited in a
mound of quicklime in the crypt of the Cathedral.
Moreover, Jasper has made himself acquainted with
the route which he is to take : he has ascended and
descended the staircase, and has noted the places where
Durdles stumbled : he has observed the effects produced upon Durdles by the strong drink : having, no
doubt, already taken an impression of the key of the
iron gate, he has now taken one of the key of the
crypt : somewhere in the crypt he has discovered a
heap of quicklime.   In short, with Durdles for *corpus
vile*, Jasper has rehearsed in all its details "the journey,"

that is to say, the ascent of the tower, which he is to make with Edwin on the following Saturday, Dec. 24. "The expedition" of Dec. 19 is then for us no longer "unaccountable."

On the other hand, if Edwin was to be attacked in the Close or in the churchyard, and his body was to be hidden in the Sapsea monument, it is not easy to see why Jasper should make a careful study of the tower. Mr Lang indeed suggests that "it is for the purpose of discovering whether the coast be clear or not, that Jasper climbs the tower," *Puzzle*, p. 20 : it is not until Jasper "has made sure of the utterly deserted character of the area by observations from the tower top" that he can venture "to convey several wheel-barrowfuls of quicklime from Durdles' yard to Mrs Sapsea's sepulchre." For myself, I do not understand how observations made from the top of the tower could give Jasper any assurance that he will not be seen in the churchyard, and I demur altogether to the hypothesis which Mr Lang shares with Mr Proctor, that Jasper brought quicklime in a wheelbarrow from one end of Cloisterham to the other. Any one who is acquainted with Rochester will perceive that the route through the Monks' Vineyard would have dangers as great as those of the route along the High Street, though no doubt of a different kind.

(5) In the narrative of the events of Dec. 24, ch. xiv, we are told, p. 172, that "the mere mechanism of Jasper's throat is a little tender, for he wears, both with his singing-robe and with his ordinary dress, a large black scarf of strong close-woven silk, slung

loosely round his neck": yet Crisparkle notes that he
"is in beautiful voice this day," and compliments him
upon it. Again, at p. 174, when Jasper goes to join
his guests, "he pauses for an instant…to pull off that
great black scarf, and hang it in a loop upon his arm.
For that brief time, his face is knitted and stern."
That this "large black scarf of strong close-woven
silk" was important, Sir Luke Fildes immediately
recognised (Mr W. R. Hughes, quoted by Mr Walters,
Clues, p. 38): and I have no doubt whatever that the
expositors are right in making it the instrument of
the crime. But I dispute Mr Lang's contention, p. 41,
that, if Jasper strangled, or rather, tried to strangle,
Drood with the scarf, those phrases in ch. xxiii which
imply a fall from a height can have no reference to the
attempted murder, and are therefore prophetic of what
is to come on the day of retribution. On the contrary,
it seems to me that Jasper, if he intended to fling or
push his nephew down the steep, narrow, staircase of
the Cathedral tower, would throw the scarf over his
victim's head; and that when, having thus precluded
"struggle, consciousness of peril, entreaty," he proceeded to remove the lifeless or apparently lifeless body
from the foot of the staircase to the heap of quicklime
in the crypt, the scarf would have a further utility.

My theory is then, in brief, as follows. When Drood
returned to the gatehouse not long after midnight on
Christmas Eve, Jasper, having hospitably pressed upon
him some of his "good stuff," proposed a visit to the
Cathedral tower, and Drood was nothing loth. As they
descended the staircase of the tower, Jasper threw his

scarf over Drood's head, and, having thus silenced, blinded, and disabled, him, pushed him down the steep stairs[1]. Drood, if he was not killed, was stunned by the fall. Jasper dragged the body into the crypt, and, having removed from it the watch and the shirt-pin, buried it in the heap of quicklime.

It will be seen that in this statement I am careful not to assume that Edwin is dead : for, though I find it difficult to imagine the manner of his escape, I recognise that Dickens may have a surprise in store for us, and I know that others who are better acquainted with his manner than I am are strongly of opinion that this is so. There is however one thing of which I am very sure : Grewgious did not at this point come upon the scene, hear from Edwin his story, and receive the betrothal ring again into his keeping. For, first, as has been seen, Grewgious was not at Cloisterham ; secondly, however lamely Edwin might tell his tale, it must needs have come out, that, after he left Landless, he had been in Jasper's company, whilst the rest of the extant narrative suggests that, though Grewgious has reasons for distrusting, disliking, and even hating, Jasper, he has at present nothing which

---

[1] On the morning of Christmas Day, workmen, led by Durdles, went aloft to ascertain the extent of the damage done by the storm upon the summit of the great tower. I should like to know whether Durdles noticed anything unusual in the staircase or in the crypt. I fancy that he found traces of the crime ; but, in consequence of the alarm raised by Jasper, failed to appreciate their importance, and for the moment told no one of them. If he afterwards took Datchery into his confidence, Datchery would see the significance of the story.

directly connects him with Drood's disappearance ;
thirdly, I cannot believe that Grewgious would have
suffered Landless to remain under suspicion, when it
was easy to clear him ; fourthly, I do not see why
Grewgious, having recovered the ring, should not at
once make use of it for the conviction of the would-be
murderer.

Here then for the present I leave the study of
Jasper's machinations against Edwin Drood.

§ iv. *Jasper's machinations against Neville Landless: chapters xv—xvii and xix—xxii.*

Jasper's scheme, as now finally arranged, is then to make away with Drood in such a manner that Neville will be suspected of having murdered him. Accordingly in ch. xv, when Neville is pursued and arrested, Jasper studiously aggravates the case against him. Then comes the news that Edwin and Rosa have broken off their engagement. Hereupon Jasper withdraws, for the moment, the suggestion that Edwin has been murdered: "he may have disappeared of his own accord, and may yet be alive and well," p. 190. The next day however Crisparkle discovers Drood's watch and shirt-pin at the Weir, placed there, presumably, by Jasper: and, when at length Neville is released and leaves Cloisterham, Jasper shows Crisparkle an entry in his diary in which he affirms his conviction, based upon Crisparkle's discovery of the watch and shirt-pin, that Drood has been murdered, and solemnly records his intention of fastening the crime upon the murderer, p. 197. In short, having disposed of Drood, Jasper now intrigues against his other rival.

In the narrative outlined in the foregoing paragraph there is an incident which, though, so far as

I know, the expositors have neglected it, seems to call for comment.   On leaving Grewgious and Jasper, Crisparkle "walked to Cloisterham Weir."   "He often did so, and consequently there was nothing remarkable in his footsteps tending that way.   But the preoccupation of his mind so hindered him from planning any walk, or taking heed of the objects he passed, that his first consciousness of being near the Weir was derived from the sound of the falling water close at hand. 'How did I come here!' was his first thought, as he stopped.   'Why did I come here!' was his second. Then he stood intently listening to the water.   A familiar passage in his reading, about airy tongues that syllable men's names, rose so unbidden to his ear, that he put it from him with his hand, as if it were tangible."   Surely Crisparkle thinks of the familiar quotation because, in answer to his two questions— "How did I come here!" "Why did I come here!"— he seems to hear a man's name, the name of John Jasper.   Now we know already that Jasper has an uncanny faculty of hypnotic suggestion, which he seeks to exercise upon Rosa: see in particular pp. 74, 79[1]. We are, I think, to understand that, having already left the watch and shirt-pin at the Weir, he now uses his mesmeric power to send Crisparkle to find them there.   He has planned this before Crisparkle arrives. Hence it is that, when Grewgious tells him of the rupture of the engagement, he can afford to find in the

---

[1] Mr J. W. Wilson (*Dickensian*, iv, 103) notes Jasper's mesmeric power, but apparently has not observed that it explains Crisparkle's visits to the Weir on December 27, 28.

news "crumbs of comfort": Crisparkle's discovery of the watch and shirt-pin will justify him in resuming his operations against Neville.

And now half a year passes, and the interest in Drood's disappearance begins to die away. When the story is resumed, we find Neville established at Staple Inn under the eye of Grewgious. Jasper has taken a room there, and keeps an ostentatious watch upon Neville, "which," says Crisparkle, "would not only of itself haunt and torture his life, but would expose him to the torment of a perpetually reviving suspicion, whatever he might do, or wherever he might go," p. 209; compare p. 253. Meanwhile, in ch. xix, Jasper seeks to compel Rosa's acceptance of his addresses by telling her that it is his intention to fasten the death of Edwin upon Neville: "It was hawked through the late inquiries by Mr Crisparkle, that young Landless had confessed to him that he was a rival of my lost boy. That is an inexpiable offence in my eyes. The same Mr Crisparkle knows under my hand that I have devoted myself to the murderer's discovery and destruction, be he whom he might, and that I determined to discuss the mystery with no one until I should hold the clue in which to entangle the murderer as in a net. I have since worked patiently to wind and wind it round him; and it is slowly winding as I speak."…"Circumstances may accumulate so strongly *even against an innocent man*, that directed, sharpened, and pointed, they may slay him. One wanting link discovered by perseverance against a guilty man, proves his guilt, however slight its evidence before, and he dies. Young Landless stands in deadly peril either way," pp. 226, 227.

Thus in this second act of the drama Jasper is plotting against Neville with a ferocity as great as that which he had shown against Edwin in the first act : and, when Rosa flies to Staple Inn, she comes to Grewgious, not, to tell him that she has begun to suspect Jasper of the murder of his nephew, but, to ask Grewgious for protection for herself, and to warn him of the intrigue against Neville, p. 236. Accordingly, the next morning, July 4, it is decided that Rosa shall remain in London, and that Tartar shall visit Neville openly and often, in the hope that, "if the purpose really is to isolate Neville from all friends and acquaintance and wear his daily life out grain by grain," Jasper will enter into communications with Tartar and thus show his hand, p. 253. In a word, the purpose of the Staple Inn alliance is, not, to penetrate the mystery of Edwin's disappearance, but, to protect Rosa and Neville.

Nevertheless, it will be well to collect such notices as Dickens has given us of the attitude of the allies towards the mystery of Edwin Drood. Rosa, pp. 232, 233, suspects Jasper of having murdered Edwin, but distrusts her suspicion and keeps it to herself. That suspicion "appeared to have no harbour in Mr Crisparkle's imagination," p. 270. "If it ever haunted Helena's thoughts or Neville's, neither gave it one spoken word of utterance," p. 270. "Mr Grewgious took no pains to conceal his implacable dislike of Jasper, yet he never referred it, however distantly, to

J.

3

such a source," p. 270.   It may be worth while to add
that Grewgious' dislike of Jasper dates from the preceding Christmas.   For, whereas in the conversation
early in December, ch. ix, Grewgious betrays neither
suspicion nor coldness, when they meet again on the
night of December 27, p. 183, Grewgious is "curt,"
"cool," "exasperating," "provokingly slow," in telling
his news, and his refusal of Jasper's invitation to eat
with him, p. 188, is a hardly veiled insult.   But there
is nothing to show whether Grewgious' present abhor-
rence of Jasper is caused by the disappearance of
Drood or by something independent of it.   It is
possible, that Grewgious has heard from the two girls
enough about Jasper's feelings towards Rosa to suspect him of having murdered his rival : but it is also
conceivable that something wholly independent of
the Cloisterham mystery has satisfied Grewgious that
Jasper is "a brigand and a wild beast in combination,"
p. 253.

It would seem then that, whatever the several
members of the Staple Inn alliance may privately
think about Edwin's disappearance, no one of them
has broached to any other the suspicion that he has
been made away with by Jasper.   This being so, it is
quite certain that no two of them have set a watch upon
Jasper at Cloisterham in the hope of penetrating the
mystery of Edwin's disappearance.   Again, Grewgious
knows what Jasper means him to know, namely, that
Neville is watched at Staple Inn : but, until Rosa
arrives on the night of July 3 with the story of her
talk with Jasper on the afternoon of that day, there is

nothing beyond conjecture to explain Jasper's policy
in regard to Neville, and nothing whatever to show
that his persecution of Rosa is not at an end.   Accordingly, at the conference on July 4, the defence of
Neville and Rosa appears to be discussed as a *res
integra*.   We cannot then suppose that, in the interest
of Neville and Rosa, Grewgious has already sent an
agent to observe Jasper's doings at Cloisterham.

Yet, between ch. xvii, which recounts how Crisparkle visited Grewgious and Neville on June 30,
and ch. xix, which describes the stormy conversation
between Rosa and Jasper on July 3, we have a chapter
headed "A settler in Cloisterham," which tells how,
"at about this time," that is to say, June 30 or July 1,
"Mr Datchery" established himself in Mrs Tope's
lodgings with the intention, made quite clear to the
reader, of watching Jasper at Cloisterham.   Further,
Datchery, whoever he may be, does not represent the
opium-woman, who for reasons not known to us is also
on the watch; for in ch. xxiii Datchery observes her
gestures with surprise and amazement: and, if he does
not represent the opium-woman, his point of view
must needs be that of Grewgious and his friends.
Yet, as has been seen, before July 4 Grewgious and
his friends can hardly have taken the field, either
offensively with a view to the discovery of the murderer
or would-be murderer of Edwin Drood, or defensively
with a view to the protection of Neville and Rosa.   In
a word, Datchery seems to be a representative or
agent of the Staple Inn allies; but it is inconceivable
that they should have had a representative or agent at

Cloisterham on Friday June 30 or Saturday July 1. On the other hand, the appearance of such a representative or agent on any day subsequent to the Staple Inn conference, say on July 5 or July 6, is exactly what we should expect. Let us suppose that, while Tartar will get into touch with Jasper when he visits Staple Inn, Datchery, whoever he may be, is to observe Jasper's movements when he is at Cloisterham. This is an intelligible scheme; whereas the conference is strangely ineffective, if its sole result is that Tartar is told off to verify Crisparkle's conjectural explanation of Jasper's visits to Staple Inn, especially as that explanation has now been justified by Jasper's words to Rosa.

But if the tenour of the principal narrative forces upon us, as I think it does, the conviction that the episode contained in ch. xviii is subsequent to the events recorded in chs. xix to xxii, the awkward facts remain that ch. xviii, "A settler in Cloisterham," is interposed between ch. xvii and chs. xix to xxii, and that the opening words "At about this time" should mean, not "about July 5 or 6," but "about June 30 or July 1." How is the discrepancy to be explained?

My conviction is that ch. xviii has been introduced prematurely, that is to say, that it ought to have followed ch. xxii; and that if Dickens had lived to issue the fifth and sixth monthly instalments, he would have placed our ch. xviii, without the alteration of a single word, after ch. xxii, next before ch. xxiii.

This will seem an audacious hypothesis. There is, however, a tradition which seems to show that Dickens was aware of the oversight. Forster tells us, *Life*, iii, 429 f., that "Dickens had become a little nervous about the course of the tale, from a fear that he might have plunged too soon into the incidents leading on to the catastrophe, such as the Datchery assumption in the fifth number (a misgiving he had certainly expressed to his sister-in-law)." Dickens may well have been nervous about the future organisation of a difficult story which had to be cut up into lengths for periodical publication : but I suspect that his "misgiving" about "the Datchery assumption" was due to the discovery, not that there was any error in the structure of the story, for there was none, but that in telling it he had introduced Datchery some five days too soon. If, as appears, Dickens was in the habit of reading what he had written to his friends, he would perceive, as soon as he came to ch. xix, that ch. xviii was out of place.

In short, I suppose the chronology of these chapters to be as follows. On Friday, June 30, Crisparkle visits Grewgious and Neville, ch. xvii. On Saturday, July 1, Miss Twinkleton's school breaks up. On Monday, July 3, Helena comes to London, and Rosa, after her talk with Jasper, follows her, chs. xix, xx. On Tuesday, July 4, Crisparkle and Tartar appear, and the Staple Inn conference is held, chs. xxi, xxii. Then, on Wednesday, July 5, or Thursday, July 6, Datchery begins his watch at Cloisterham, ch. xviii : and in ch. xxiii he continues it.

§ v. *Datchery: chapters xviii and xxiii.*

We have seen that "at about this time,"—that is to say, if the chapter called "A settler in Cloisterham" is correctly placed between ch. xvii and ch. xix, about June 30 or July 1, but, if I am right in my contention that this chapter should immediately precede ch. xxiii, about July 5 or July 6,—one Dick Datchery established himself at Cloisterham. Ostensibly he is "a single buffer" who proposes to make a home for himself there: but from the outset the reader is allowed to see that the newcomer's business is to watch Jasper and to collect information about him. The conversations with Mrs Tope, p. 216, with Sapsea, pp. 218, 219, and with the opium-woman, pp. 280 ff., prove Datchery's keen interest in Jasper and his doings. The "change of countenance," "the sudden look," and "the reddening," pp. 282, 283, suggest that at this point Datchery suspects that the opium-woman may have something to tell: and her gestures in the cathedral and the few sentences exchanged after the service, pp. 286, 287, assure him that he is not mistaken.

But who is Datchery? Is he, as a writer in the *Cornhill Magazine*, March 1884, supposes, an ordinary detective, employed in the course of business by Grewgious? Or, is he an extraordinary detective, some one who has his private reasons for desiring to unravel the plot? I cannot think that he is any ordinary detective: for (1) whereas the ordinary detective would naturally seek to lose himself in the crowd, Datchery is unusual, eccentric, conspicuous; (2) the ample wig is plainly a disguise, and Datchery's forgetfulness of it seems to indicate that he is not in the habit of disguising himself; (3) his whole bearing is that of a principal and not of a subordinate. Let us suppose then that he is an extraordinary detective, some one personally interested in the case. Now "the moderate stroke" which he scores up in his cupboard, p. 285, after his first conversation with the opium-woman, suggests that he has hitherto known nothing about her and her acquaintance with Jasper, and that as yet he is not sure that her curiosity is in any way significant. On the other hand, "the thick line added to the score, extending from the top of the cupboard door to the bottom," p. 287, implies, not only that the old woman's animosity against Jasper is to Datchery a discovery, but also that it seems to him an important fact. Thus Datchery has hitherto known nothing about Jasper's hidden life, not even as much as Dickens has disclosed to his readers in the first chapter: whence it appears that Datchery comes to the inquiry, not, as the opium-woman seems to do, from the point of view of Jasper's past, but, like Grewgious and his allies, from the point of view of Jasper's present. Now, if Dickens has dealt fairly with us, we know by this time all the people who are directly interested in the Cloisterham mystery. If, besides the personages who have been introduced to us, there had been any one else directly interested in it, we should at any rate have heard of him. But we know of no one of the sort, and therefore I conclude that the extraordinary detective, personally interested in the case, who comes to it from the point of view of the Cloisterham mystery, must needs be some one who is already on the stage.

Now a genius may masquerade as a fool and a courtier as a clown : but a fool cannot at will play the part of a genius, nor a clown that of a courtier. As Aristotle might say, capacity can ape incapacity, but incapacity cannot ape capacity. This being so, I am sure that Bazzard, who is not only "particularly angular," p. 102, but also somnolent, dull, incompetent, egotistical, is wholly incapable of playing the part of the supple, quick-witted, resolute, dignified, Datchery. So I confidently reject the theory of the ingenious authors of *John Jasper's Secret*, that Datchery is Bazzard[1].

Grewgious, no doubt, has both resolution and ability. But the man who is constitutionally cautious,

[1] Since this was written, Mr Edwin Charles, in his *Keys to the Edwin Drood Mystery*, has sketched a conclusion for the story on the hypothesis that Datchery is Bazzard. The objection—to my mind the fatal objection—is that Mr Charles' Bazzard, who directs the campaign against Jasper, is not the somnolent, dull, incompetent, egotistical, Bazzard to whom Dickens has introduced us. It may well be that Grewgious is employing Bazzard in the subordinate task of obtaining facts about Jasper's past history.

and consciously, though perhaps only superficially, "angular," does not suddenly become ready, adroit, and versatile. Moreover, his business detains him in town; and he presently finds work to do for the common cause in watching Jasper's appearances at Staple Inn. Hence, Datchery is not Grewgious.

Nor can I think that Edwin Drood, if still alive, is capable of this great rôle. Boyish, kindly, and, so far as his limitations permit, considerate, he has neither the intellect nor the will nor the address of Datchery; see pp. 26, 38, 114, 152, 169. He differs from Datchery as a schoolboy differs from a diplomatist. In the parting with Rosa we see Edwin "at his best," and the discovery of Jasper's treachery might have a stimulating effect upon his character and intelligence: but it could not raise him above "his best," it could not evoke qualities in which he is conspicuously deficient. For this reason, to say nothing of others, I confidently reject the theory of Mr Proctor and Mr Lang that Datchery is Drood.

Again, Datchery is not Tartar. For, first, at the Staple Inn conference duties are assigned to Tartar which will keep him constantly in town: "If Mr Tartar would call to see him" [Neville] "openly and often" says Helena, p. 253; "if he would spare a minute for the purpose, frequently; if he would even do so, almost daily; something might come of it." Secondly, Tartar does not possess the knowledge of Cloisterham and the Drood mystery which Datchery ought to possess and actually possesses. Thirdly, I doubt whether the cheery, straightforward, simple-minded,

Tartar is capable of Datchery's versatility, subtlety, and address[1].

Nor is Datchery Neville Landless. For, in their consideration for his feelings, the allies have not admitted him to their deliberations, and are hardly likely to make him their principal agent.

In fact, to use Bazzard's phrase, I "follow" Mr Walters in his demonstration, pp. 51—59, that Datchery is not Bazzard, Drood, or Grewgious, and in his corollary, that, with the exception of Helena Landless, none of the personages already on the stage is capable of this exacting rôle. This part of Mr Walters' argument seems to me so cogent and so lucidly expressed that I am content with this barest possible statement of the reasons for my acceptance of it.

Again, I "follow" Mr Walters in much of his positive argument for the identification of Datchery with Helena. In my opinion (*a*) such phrases as the author's "Let whomsoever it most concerned look well to it!" p. 79, and Helena's "Not under any circumstances" in reply to Edwin's "You would be afraid of him, under similar circumstances, wouldn't you, Miss Landless?" p. 74, indicate that Dickens meant Helena to take a prominent part in defending Neville and Rosa and in unmasking Jasper; (*b*) Dickens has been studiously careful to endow Helena with the resolution, the presence of mind, and the address, which Datchery requires for his task, and possesses in

---

[1] For an excellent presentation of "the case for Tartar," see Mr G. F. Gadd's paper with this title in the *Dickensian*, ii, 13.

perfection; (*c*) when once Jasper has declared his hostility to Neville, Helena would not be the Helena who is described to us at p. 207 and elsewhere, if she did not take the field in Neville's defence. These are the considerations which principally weigh with me in at any rate a provisional acceptance of Mr Walters' original and attractive conjecture.

Nevertheless there are some of Mr Walters' "proofs" which I should not care to insist upon, and there are others which seem to me to break down. Thus, (*a*) whereas Mr Walters thinks that Datchery's mismanagement of his head-gear proves him to be a woman, *Clues*, pp. 63—65, I doubt whether it establishes more than that Datchery wore a wig, and was an amateur detective, unaccustomed to disguise: (*b*) whereas Mr Walters, *Clues*, p. 81, supposes Datchery to call on Mrs Tope and not on Mr Tope because "a woman would prefer to call on another woman," he forgets that at p. 214 the waiter has spoken of *Mrs* Tope as having "once upon a time let lodgings or offered to let them," and has referred to Mr Tope, not as letting lodgings, but only as connected with the Cathedral: (*c*) I cannot think with Mr Walters, *Clues*, p. 83, that Datchery scored in chalk because "the woman would have been betrayed by her penmanship"; surely Datchery, whether male or female, might represent results graphically: (*d*) whereas Mr Walters, *Clues*, p. 85, argues that "Dickens does not represent Helena and Jasper as exchanging a single word," so that her "rich and low" tones were not familiar to him, the story of the dinner party in

ch. vii, see especially p. 74, hardly warrants Mr Walters'
"strange fact": (*e*) whereas Mr Walters, *Clues*, pp. 78,
79, regards Grewgious' doubtful reply, p. 242, to Rosa's
"I may go to Helena to-morrow?" as an admission
that Helena was not then at Staple Inn, Grewgious'
hesitation, explained p. 247, is, as Mr Lang, *Puzzle*,
p. 39, points out, perfectly reasonable, and ceases the
next day, only because, by the help of Tartar, the two
girls can now meet without Jasper's knowledge. These
arguments then I set aside as inconclusive: but if, as I
think, they do not help Mr Walters' case, neither do
they prejudice it.

There is however another of Mr Walters' proofs
which may, I think, be turned against him with deadly
effect; and indeed, if properly enlarged and justified,
might even *seem* to be conclusive against the Datchery-
Helena theory.   Commenting on the conversation
between Helena and Rosa in ch. xxii, see especially
p. 253, Mr Walters, *Clues*, p. 80, writes as follows:

"Helena's conduct at this point is also worth scrutinising. She
at once conceives a scheme for checkmating Jasper, and pertinently
inquires whether 'it would be best to wait until any more maligning
and pursuing of Neville on the part of this wretch shall disclose
itself, or to try to anticipate it?' She is in full activity. She is
prepared, not to begin operations, but to conclude them if necessary.
Dickens at this point had revealed her hand, and then, for the rest
of the story, he spirits her away. After this important conference
Helena Landless vanishes from the story. But Dick Datchery
reappears in Cloisterham!"

That is to say, Mr Walters supposes that, when
Helena has already begun operations at Cloisterham
in the character of Datchery, she is in London, and

tells Rosa to send Crisparkle to ask Grewgious whether
"it would be best to try to anticipate" Jasper's pursuit
of Neville, "so far as to find out whether any such
goes on darkly about us": Grewgious enthusiastically
assents: Helena arranges with Rosa that Tartar shall
visit Neville: the girls part: "Dick Datchery reappears in Cloisterham." Seemingly Mr Walters
regards this as a consistent scheme. I do not. The
words used by Mr Walters himself are noteworthy:
"She at once conceives a scheme for checkmating
Jasper." If "she at once conceives a scheme," she has
not already conceived it: and it must be remembered
that she could not have conceived it sooner; for it was
only on the previous afternoon that Jasper, in his
interview with Rosa, had used the threatening words
which suggest Helena's inquiry, and it was only on
this very morning that Helena heard of them from
Rosa. Yet, according to Mr Walters, Helena has
already been doing at Cloisterham in the character of
Datchery exactly what she now for the first time
resolves to do. The truth is that, if Datchery is
already at work at Cloisterham, he is not Helena:
and that if Datchery is Helena, she does not begin
work at Cloisterham till after the conference at Staple
Inn on July 4[1].

[1] It is worth while to note that exactly this argument is used by
Mr Walters to show (a) that Datchery is not Grewgious; "Datchery
appeared in Cloisterham *before* Mr Grewgious knew from Rosa's
own lips how serious the state of affairs had become, and how
necessary it was to keep a close watch upon Jasper," *Clues*, p. 56:
and (b) that Datchery is not Bazzard, *Clues*, p. 52; "But if Grewgious
had given him" [Bazzard] "this task, and been credulous enough to

When I first read Mr Walters' *Clues*, this objection to the Datchery-Helena theory seemed to me insuperable. Everything else appeared to designate Helena for Datchery's task; but if Datchery was watching Jasper at pp. 213—221, before Helena received the information which led her at p. 253 to suggest setting a watch, how could Datchery be Helena? And when I proceeded to work out the chronology of the story, I felt the difficulty all the more. On Friday, June 30, pp. 206, 207, Crisparkle implies that Helena has been, and still is, at Cloisterham, living her usual life, and he says explicitly that next week she will join Neville at Staple Inn, apparently for a long visit. Accordingly on Monday, July 3, she comes to town. Now if Helena was at Miss Twinkleton's on Friday and came to town on the following Monday, this leaves barely three days in which she could have played the part of Datchery. Plainly the time is too short, even for a preliminary reconnaissance. Moreover, as we know, Datchery proposes "to take a lodging in the picturesque old city for a month or two." Thus, once more, if Datchery is already at work, he is not Helena.

But if, as in the preceding chapter I have endeavoured to show, Datchery did not appear at

think him capable of performing it, he could not have sent him to Cloisterham until after he had heard Rosa's story of Jasper's perfidy. Yet Datchery had been in Cloisterham before that time—that is, before either Grewgious or Bazzard knew of the urgent need for placing Jasper under supervision." Now if this argument is good to show that Datchery is neither Grewgious nor Bazzard, it is equally good to show that Datchery is not Helena. It is a little strange that Mr Walters has overlooked this obvious criticism.

Cloisterham till after the Staple Inn conference on Tuesday, July 4, the identification of Datchery with Helena presents no difficulty whatever. In ch. xvii Crisparkle and Neville talk of Helena as still, Friday, June 30, at Cloisterham, but as about to join Neville in London on Monday, July 3, for a long stay, and Grewgious shows Crisparkle that Jasper is on the watch at Staple Inn. In ch. xix Jasper frightens Rosa with his wild threats. In ch. xx Rosa flies to Grewgious. In ch. xxi Tartar appears. In ch. xxii, early on Tuesday, July 4, Rosa tells Helena of Jasper's designs against Neville, and Helena raises the question whether it would be well to try to anticipate them. Grewgious assents. The sequence of events points unmistakably to one result, namely, Helena's return to Cloisterham in disguise on July 5 or 6, to begin a watch upon Jasper's movements.

Now it can be shown that, though Helena had contemplated a long stay at Staple Inn, she left London very soon after the conference. For, unquestionably, if she had remained there, we should have heard that "the pretty girl at Billickin's" was visited by a dark girl whose occasional presence encouraged and enlivened her in "the gritty state of things." As we hear of nothing of the sort, we may be quite sure that Helena is no longer in town. And there is another proof of this. When the serious business of the conference is over, Rosa in answer to a question tells Helena that she will not go back to Miss Twinkleton's at Cloisterham, and that her guardian will take care of her. Hereupon Helena inquires: "And I shall hear

of my Rosebud from Mr Tartar ?"   Now, if Helena is
to hear of Rosa from Tartar, and Tartar and Rosa are
to be in town, surely Helena has made up her mind to
leave London.   And, if she is not in town, presumably
she is at Cloisterham.   What she saw and did and
said there, is, I conceive, recorded in chapters xviii
and xxiii.

Mr Walters' theory is however open to certain
objections, and I must now say something in reply
to them.   In the first place it is urged that Datchery's
manner is conspicuously unlike Helena's : "What is
most unlike the stern, fierce, sententious Helena,"
says Mr Lang, *Puzzle*, p. 37, "is Datchery's habit of
' chaffing[1].'   He fools the ass of a Mayor, Sapsea, by
most exaggerated deference : his tone is always that
of indolent mockery, which one doubts whether the
'intense' and concentrated Helena could assume."   But
if Datchery is Helena, I do not expect to find between
them resemblances of manner.   We are told that in
early days Helena had disguised herself as a boy, and
we are given to understand that she was able and
resourceful.   We are, I think, to give her credit for a
real histrionic gift.   If this is so, I expect her to invent
for Datchery a well-defined personality, wholly unlike
her own ; to supply him with a sufficiency of tricks and

[1] We know that Dickens chose "a habit of chaffing" to be the
characteristic of his detective before he determined the detective's
age and physique : for "the young man," Poker, in the rejected
chapter plays with Sapsea in the same way that Datchery does,
and uses phrases which would have been quite appropriate in the
mouth of Datchery.

mannerisms; and to sustain the part effectively and consistently. It is the bad actor, and not the good one, who on the stage betrays the characteristics of his every-day life: and it is only fair to attribute to Helena a portion of that versatility in impersonation which some of us remember as a principal feature in Dickens' acting. If Dickens could play the part of an old woman, surely he might suppose a young woman to play the part of an elderly gentleman. But, Mr Lang may say, there are limits to the actor's capabilities, and a power of "chaffing" is beyond Helena's reach. I am not so sure of it. At pp. 253, 254 she indulges more than once in a quiet, kindly, mockery of Rosa which suggests possibilities in this direction.

Again, it is objected that Datchery's meals are those of a man, and not of a woman. But, if a woman plays the part of a man, she must order what a man would order. If Datchery had not ordered a pint of sherry with his fried sole and veal cutlet, the waiter at the Crozier would have thought that there was something wrong: if Datchery had scorned "the supper of bread-and-cheese and salad and ale" Mrs Tope might have thought him strangely fastidious. In excuse for Helena it may be suggested that possibly she did not consume all that the waiter and Mrs Tope set before her. Again, it is said, Datchery is at home with Durdles, Deputy, and the opium-woman: surely this is strange, if Datchery is Helena. For myself, I cannot conceive that Helena would find it difficult to draw these people out, and I think that she does it without loss of dignity. Again, if Datchery recognises that by "Jacks" Deputy means sailors, the recognition is expressed interrogatively and conjecturally, so that it hardly implies any special familiarity with the term. Again, when, *Puzzle*, p. 46, Mr Lang asks "How could Helena, fresh from Ceylon, know the old tavern way of keeping scores," may we not suppose that she had seen it in use in her country walks with Neville?

Then too it is represented that Helena, with her knowledge of Cloisterham, could not have gone "boggling about and about the Cathedral Tower," p. 214, when she was looking for Mrs Tope's. This objection seems to rest upon a misconception of Datchery's conversation with the waiter at the Crozier. When Datchery invites the waiter to recommend him "a fair lodging for a single buffer": "something old... something odd and out of the way; something venerable, architectural, and inconvenient": and, finally, asks whether there is "anything Cathedrally," it is quite plain that Datchery—whoever he may be—knows, or knows of, Mrs Tope's lodgings, and is determined to make the waiter recommend them. The waiter's thoughts do not travel quickly : but the word "Cathedrally" suggests to him that "Mr Tope would be the likeliest party to inform in that line," and his mention of Mr Tope reminds him that Mrs Tope used to advertise lodgings. In the same way, Datchery is quite familiar with the gatehouse, though he deliberately plays the part of a stranger, and "boggling about and about the Cathedral Tower," does not arrive at his destination until he has made acquaintance with Deputy and obtained his assistance. In the same way, Datchery

is careful not to know too much about the tragedy of
the preceding Christmas and to listen respectfully to
Mrs Tope's corrections of his ideas about it. Plainly
Datchery has much more local knowledge than he
admits himself to possess : so that there is nothing in
all this which conflicts with Mr Walters' theory.

Then too I am asked, If Datchery is Helena, and
therefore already knows the gatehouse, why does she,
p. 215, give it "a second look of some interest?"
Surely it is because it now has for her a new importance. Hitherto it has been no more than the
home of a man whom she dislikes and distrusts. It is
now the object upon which her thoughts are concentrated : to watch it is to be her business for weeks and
perhaps for months. In the same way, at p. 283, we
read—"John Jasper's lamp is kindled, and his light-
house is shining when Mr Datchery returns alone
towards it. As mariners on a dangerous voyage, approaching an iron-bound coast, may look along the
beams of the warning light to the haven lying beyond
it that may never be reached, so Mr Datchery's wistful
gaze is directed to this beacon, and beyond." In other
words, Helena, whose interest in the case is not that of
a professional detective, is profoundly conscious that
the well-being of those who are dear to her depends
upon her success in fathoming and counteracting the
schemes of Jasper. In short, "the second look" and
"the wistful glance" are not Datchery's: they are rare
revelations of the true Helena.

How much then has Helena achieved? In the
language of the cricketer, she has "played herself in."

That is to say, she has established herself in Mrs Tope's unoccupied rooms from which she can watch the goings in and goings out of Jasper and his visitors: she has become in the character of Datchery a familiar figure in the streets of Cloisterham: she is "the chartered bore of the city," p. 281: in particular, she has made acquaintance as Datchery with the waiter at the Crozier, Deputy, Mrs Tope, Jasper, the Mayor, Durdles, and doubtless others. This is much. At the end of her first day in Cloisterham she is already justified, p. 221, in congratulating herself upon "a rather busy after-noon." This however is as far as she has gone in ch. xviii. But in ch. xxiii she has two experiences which seem to her noteworthy. The first is a meeting with the opium-woman, who comes to Cloisterham in pursuit of Jasper, follows him to the gatehouse, and asks Datchery to tell her Jasper's name and calling. She may see and hear Mr John Jasper, says Datchery, if she goes to the Cathedral at seven o'clock in the morning. But all that concerns John Jasper concerns Dick Datchery. So Datchery walks with the old woman as far as the Monks' Vineyard, and hears from her how on the preceding Christmas Eve a young gentleman called Edwin, who had no sweetheart, had given her money with which to buy opium. At the mention of opium, "Mr Datchery, with a sudden change of countenance, gives her a sudden look": and, on hear-ing Edwin's name, he "drops some money, stoops to pick it up, and reddens with the exertion." Plainly the stranger's reference to opium and her knowledge of Edwin's name surprise Datchery. So Datchery tells

Deputy to find out where the old woman lives in London. But a moderate stroke is all that can be added to the score. The next morning however, when the old woman grins and shakes her fist at the choirmaster, and presently affirms that she knows him "better far than all the Reverend Parsons put together know him," Datchery "adds one thick line to the score, extending from the top of the cupboard door to the bottom." Why does Datchery thus distinguish? The reason is, I think, that, whereas the questions put by the old woman on the preceding evening might mean nothing more than idle curiosity, her gestures at the morning service show that she knows Jasper, and hates him with a hatred which is perhaps all the more noteworthy because it has nothing to do either with Jasper's persecution of Rosa or with the disappearance of Edwin Drood. What Datchery has learnt is then that there is a keenly interested watcher who is not commissioned by the Staple Inn alliance. It will be worth while, thinks Datchery, to get into touch with such an one; or at any rate to discover the motive of her animosity. Of course we, who have been permitted to listen to the ramblings of Jasper, know that Datchery is not wrong in so thinking; for the old woman has information which would be invaluable to the allies: but Datchery has no assurance that it is so, and, for the moment, the long, thick, line indicates nothing more than hopeful expectation.

How then will Datchery go to work? Conjecture will not carry us very far. But it is obvious to suppose that sooner or later Datchery will win the old woman's confidence, and will hear from her of her grievance, of the watch which she has kept upon Jasper in her den, and of the mutterings which have betrayed to her his recent misdeeds. We know further that Datchery intends to visit Durdles, and that Deputy is to be of the party, p. 221. Presumably, "the unaccountable journey" will be repeated ; and it is easy to guess that the two vagabonds will find a more sympathetic companion in Datchery than they had done in Jasper. Probably, they will both have something important to tell about the preceding Christmas Eve. Had Durdles perhaps already found in the quicklime of the crypt the ring which, according to Forster, was to identify the person murdered, the locality of the crime, and the man who committed it ? The expositors have seen that these results might be obtained if an advertisement were to be published, offering a reward for a betrothal ring known to have been in the possession of the late Edwin Drood at the time of his disappearance. The criminal would come to recover what in his ignorance he had not removed from the body, and might be apprehended, or at any rate identified, by watchers placed for the purpose where the ring had been found. So much seems highly probable.

No. IV.]   JULY, 1870.   [Price One Shilling.

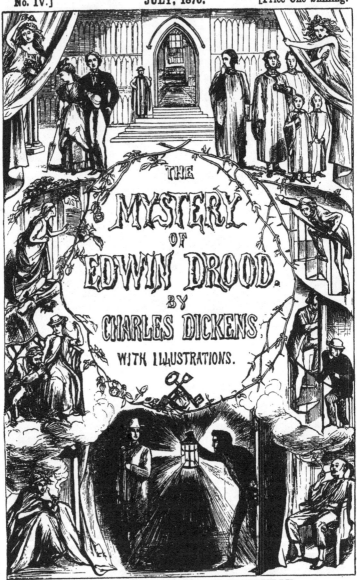

THE
MYSTERY
OF
EDWIN DROOD.
BY
CHARLES DICKENS
WITH ILLUSTRATIONS.

LONDON: CHAPMAN & HALL, 193, PICCADILLY.

Advertisements to be sent to the Publishers, and ADAMS & FRANCIS, 59, Fleet Street, E.C.
[The right of Translation is reserved.]

§ vi. *The cover.*

It may be thought that any one who goes out of his way to write about *The Mystery* is bound to interpret the pictures which appear on the cover of the original issue, and therefore I proceed to say what I think about them. But I cannot feel as much confidence as Mr Lang and Mr Walters do in this evidence. It is to be remembered that, when the cover was designed, Dickens had not written even so much of the story as is extant, and did not himself know the details of the scenes selected for presentation. Hence, when Mr Lang argues that the lower of the two pictures on the left side does not represent Jasper's proposal to Rosa, because in the story "he stands apart, leaning on a sundial," *Puzzle*, p. 82, the discrepancy does not seem to me decisive. Nor have I complete confidence in Mr Collins' ability to distinguish adequately in these thumb-nail sketches the several personalities which Dickens had more or less accurately described to him. Finally, it must not be forgotten that we are prejudiced and hampered by our familiarity with Sir L. Fildes' effective designs drawn, as it would seem, with a complete knowledge of the corresponding text.

There are however some certainties and some probabilities. We may fairly presume that the figures in the four corners represent comedy, tragedy, the opium-woman, and the Chinaman. In the nave of the Cathedral, Edwin and Rosa pair off against Jasper and Crisparkle. Despite the discrepancy which Mr Lang points out, I think that the lower of the two pictures on our left shows Jasper and Rosa in the garden of the Nuns' House. In the upper side-piece, the girl is, I am sure, Rosa flying from Jasper's pursuit, in full view of a placard announcing Edwin's disappearance. It is true that the hatless girl with her hair streaming down her back does not answer very well to Dickens' description of Rosa, and has no resemblance to Sir L. Fildes' pictures of her: but if Dickens, when he had not yet thought out his conception of her personality, told Collins to draw a frightened girl of seventeen running away from school, no more than this could be expected. For the scheme of the sketch, compare the picture in *Bleak House,* which shows Lady Dedlock, as she mounts the staircase, turning to look at a bill announcing a reward for the discovery of the murderer of Tulkinghorn. That placards and advertisements, imploring Edwin to communicate with his uncle, had been widely circulated, we have been told at p. 182. On the right, the two men in the lower picture are, I suppose, Jasper and Durdles ascending the tower on the night of "the unaccountable expedition"; while the man above is Jasper on Christmas Eve looking down at "*that*," p. 276: "Look down, look down! You see what lies at the bottom there?" p. 274. I demur to Mr Lang's statements that the young man whom I venture to identify with Jasper is represented as "whiskerless," and that the figure which I take to be Durdles is well-dressed.

And now I come to the important vignette at the bottom of the page. According to Mr Proctor, Jasper, opening the Sapsea tomb to search for the ring, finds Edwin Drood awaiting him. "And what sees he?" asks Mr Proctor: "is it the spirit of his victim, that stands there, 'in his habit as he lived,' his hand clasped on his breast, where the ring had been[1] when he was murdered? What else can Jasper deem it? There, clearly visible in the gloom at the back of the tomb, stands Edwin Drood, with stern look fixed on him— pale, silent, relentless!" *Watched by the Dead*, p. 136. Mr Lang's comment, *Puzzle*, p. 87, is to the same effect as Mr Proctor's: "There are only two possible choices; either Collins, under Dickens's oral instructions, depicted Jasper finding Drood alive in the vault, an incident which was to occur in the story; or Dickens bade Collins do this for the purpose of misleading his readers in an illegitimate manner; while the young man in the vault was really to be some person 'made up' to look like Drood, and so to frighten Jasper with

---

[1] This picturesque detail rests upon an oversight. In the picture, the left hand is in the right-hand breast pocket: but we know from two passages in ch. xiii that Edwin used the right hand in seeking the ring, and therefore that he carried it in his left-hand breast pocket. As I have said, I attach no importance to such discrepancies: but, if Mr Proctor tries to make capital out of a supposed agreement, I may be permitted to point out that the supposed agreement is imaginary.

a pseudo-ghost of that hero. The latter device, the misleading picture, would be childish, and the pseudo-ghost, exactly like Drood, could not be acted by the gypsy-like, fierce Helena, or by any other person in the romance." According to Mr Walters, Jasper finds Datchery awaiting him.

For my own part, I suspect that the upright figure represents Drood, but that the Drood which it represents is a phantom of Jasper's imagination. Let us suppose that an advertisement for a ring known to have been in the possession of the late Edwin Drood appears in the local newspaper, and that Jasper, now for the first time aware of the ring's existence, goes to the crypt to look for it. Dickens might well suppose him at such a moment to see a vision of the murdered man, and might instruct Collins to represent what Jasper imagined himself to see. Indeed I fancy that I recognise an intentional contrast between the two figures: the one, in the foreground, full of movement, solidly drawn; the other, in the background, statuesque, and a little shadowy. Doubtless Dickens was anxious that the reader should not know too much; and if he made Collins give visible form to a hallucination of Jasper's brain, I for one do not think the procedure illegitimate. It is sad that Dickens did not live to explain the innocent deception which, as I imagine, he meant for a few months to practise upon his readers.

§ vii. *The opium-woman.*

It is quite plain that, though within the limits of the extant fragment Dickens keeps back the story of the opium-woman, he means her to play an important part in the unmasking of Jasper. So it will be worth while to collect such notices as he has vouchsafed to us about her and her doings. We know that during nine months she has been endeavouring, not without success, to make Jasper talk when under the influence of opium, p. 276, quoted above p. 17: that she has noted his threats against one Ned, called by his sweetheart Eddy, but has no personal knowledge of Drood, p. 171: that on Christmas Eve she pursues Jasper to Cloisterham, but loses him, pp. 170, 280: that she claims to "know him better far than all the Reverend Parsons put together," and hates him mortally, p. 287: that on Christmas Eve, when she saw Cloisterham for the first time, p. 282, she "wasn't so much as certain that he even went right on to the place," p. 280: and that six months later she has to ask his name and his calling, p. 280. Plainly she knows nothing of Drood or of Cloisterham: but she has a grievance of her own against Jasper, and she seeks to revenge herself upon him by discovering the crime which his mutterings under the influence of opium have partially betrayed to her. What can her grievance be?

Mr Cuming Walters offers alternative conjectures : either (*a*) the opium-woman has been deserted by Jasper's father, Jasper is her son, and "she will make the child suffer for the sins of the father, who had destroyed her happiness," *Clues*, p. 92 ; or (*b*) Jasper has "wronged a child of the woman's," *Clues*, p. 93. The former of these hypotheses is, I think, open to fatal objections : first, it is fantastic to suppose that the opium-woman seeks to revenge herself upon her dead seducer by destroying their son; secondly, the hypothesis presumes that she knows who Jasper is, whereas seemingly she knows neither his name nor where he lives. There is more to be said for the alternative hypothesis : but it seems to me unnecessary to suppose that the girl whom Jasper wronged was the child of the opium-woman. My own conjecture is that the old woman had been kindly entreated by some young girl, superior in station to herself, but inferior to Jasper : that Jasper seduced her : that his infatuation for Rosa led him to neglect his victim : that she made away with herself : and that the old woman, moved by her grateful affection for the girl, devoted herself to the pursuit of the betrayer.

And I would suggest further that the girl made away with herself on the Christmas Eve preceding that on which Edwin Drood disappeared. In the course of "the unaccountable expedition," Durdles tells Jasper that "this time last year, only a few days later," he entered the Cathedral and fell asleep. " 'And what woke me ? The ghost of a cry. The ghost of one terrific shriek, which shriek was followed by the ghost

of the howl of a dog : a long dismal woeful howl, such
as a dog gives when a person's dead. That was *my*
last Christmas Eve.' 'What do you mean?' is the
very abrupt, and one might say, fierce retort. 'I mean
that I made inquiries everywhere about, and that no
living ears but mine heard either that cry or that howl.
So I say they was both ghosts; though why they came
to me, I've never made out,'" p. 144. Now there is
nothing surprising in Durdles' illusions or dreams: for,
that the cry and the howl were illusions or dreams[1]
Durdles plainly acknowledges in the last sentence of
my extract. What is noteworthy is the effect produced
upon Jasper by the words with which Durdles con-
cludes his reminiscence—"That was *my* last Christmas
Eve." These words, with their emphasis on the possessive pronoun, seem to challenge Jasper to say what *his*
last Christmas Eve had been : and I suspect that such
conscience as he possesses is pricked by the recollection
of something which happened on that night. And I
can further conceive that the story of Jasper's previous
misconduct is the "anecdote in point," which "it would be
premature to relate," referred to by Grewgious at p. 245.
If Grewgious in collecting the rents of "the miserable
court" in which the old woman lived had heard the
pitiful story, and had connected it with Jasper, this
might account for the complete change in his attitude
towards the plausible precentor.

[1] Compare *Bleak House*, ch. xxxii, p. 419, "ghosts of sounds—
strange cracks and tickings, the rustling of garments that have no
substance in them, and the tread of dreadful feet, that would leave
no mark on the sea-sand or the winter snow."

§ viii. *Did Drood escape ?*

Thus far I have tried to collect the facts of the extant chapters; and if now and then I have wandered into the region of speculation, I have been careful to mark the tentative character of these excursions, and to limit their scope. But the time has come when I must needs say something about a speculative question which has fascinated the critics and engaged much of their attention : " Did Jasper succeed, or did he fail, in his attempt upon the life of his nephew ? "

We know (*a*) that on Christmas Eve Jasper made a premeditated attempt upon Drood's life, (*b*) that from that time Drood has not again appeared upon the scene, and (*c*) on the authority of Sir L. Fildes, that Jasper was later to be the occupant of a condemned cell : whence it is obvious to conjecture that Jasper killed Drood. But we are nowhere told so : it is possible to account otherwise for Jasper's occupation of the condemned cell : and surprise is one of the devices of the story-teller. Are we then to conclude, that, if Dickens has gone so near to saying that Jasper killed Drood without actually saying it, Drood has escaped ? No : the two contentions exactly balance one another,

Moreover, we know that Dickens is studiously keeping the issue in suspense; for one of his experimental titles for the story was—"Dead? or Alive?" Nevertheless it will be worth while to state and to consider such arguments as have been, or may be, urged in favour of either hypothesis.

That Drood escaped, is confidently maintained by Mr Proctor and Mr Lang; and I therefore rely upon them for the presentation of this theory. Their arguments are, I think, two.

First, according to Mr Proctor, "The idea which more than any other had a fascination for Dickens, and was apparently regarded by him as likely to be most potent in its influence on others, was that of a wrong-doer watched at every turn by one of whom he has no suspicion, for whom he even entertains a feeling of contempt," *Watched by the Dead*, pp. 5, 6: and "every conceivable form of his favourite theme had now been tried, save that which Dickens had himself indicated[1] as the most effective of all—that the dead should rise from the grave to confront his murderer. This idea was at length to be used, difficult though it seemed to work it out successfully," p. 22. Now, Mr Proctor has, I think, conclusively shown that "the idea of patient, unsuspected watching to bring an evil-doer to justice" was "strong in Dickens's mind," p. 11, and I recognise that *Edwin Drood* is a case in point; for both Datchery

---

[1] Apparently Mr Proctor rests this assertion upon a sentence from *Martin Chuzzlewit* which he has quoted at p. 10: "The dead man might have come out of his grave, and not confounded and appalled him so."

and the opium-woman are just such watchers.   But I
demur altogether to the corollary that, every conceivable
form of this favourite theme with one exception having
now been tried, this one exception was to be made use
of in *Edwin Drood*, and that therefore in *Edwin Drood*
the supposed victim was to be the watcher.   I am by
no means satisfied that this was the only possible varia-
tion upon the familiar theme: for, may we not think
that pursuit by two independent watchers was enough
of a novelty ?

Secondly, according to Mr Proctor, *Watched by the
Dead*, p. 71, "all the characters who die in Dickens's
stories are marked for death from the beginning," and
"there is not one note of death in aught that he"
[Drood] "does and says": and, p. 150, "there are touches
in the chapters of *Edwin Drood* preceding Edwin's
disappearance, which show any one who understands
Dickens's manner, and has an ear for the music of
his words, that Edwin Drood is not actually to be
killed, and that the Drood who is really to be seen no
more is the light-hearted whimsical[1] boy of the earlier
pages.   But that evidence was not for all readers."
Mr Lang, *Puzzle*, p. 69, endorses Mr Proctor's argument : "Mr Proctor truly adds that Edwin has none
of the signs of Dickens's doomed men, his Sidney
Cartons, and the rest.   You can tell, as it were by the
sound of the voice of Dickens, says Mr Proctor, that
Edwin is to live.   The impression is merely subjective,

---

[1] Why "whimsical"?   This is one of the last epithets which I
should apply to Edwin.   When Dickens calls Rosa "whimsical," I
understand perfectly.

but I feel the impression." "As the time approaches for Jasper's attack on him," says Mr Proctor, p. 72, "there is much in the music of the story to suggest that trouble is approaching ; but he is not to die, albeit the reader is to think him dead."

I must not transcribe the whole story of Edwin's solitary and sorrowful Christmas Eve : but I may be permitted to extract two or three paragraphs, pp. 169, 171. " He strolls about and about, to pass the time until the dinner-hour. It somehow happens that Cloisterham seems reproachful to him to-day ; has fault to find with him, as if he had not used it well ; but is far more pensive with him than angry. His wonted carelessness is replaced by a wistful looking at, and dwelling upon, all the old landmarks. He will soon be far away, and may never see them again, he thinks. Poor youth ! poor youth !"..."This is not an inspiriting close to a dull day. Alone, in a sequestered place, surrounded by vestiges of old time and decay, it rather has a tendency to call a shudder into being. He makes for the better-lighted streets, and resolves as he walks on to say nothing of this to-night, but to mention it to Jack (who alone calls him Ned), as an odd coincidence, to-morrow ; of course only as a coincidence, and not as anything better worth remembering.

" Still, it holds to him, as many things much better worth remembering never did. He has another mile or so, to linger out before the dinner-hour ; and, when he walks over the bridge and by the river, the woman's words are in the rising wind, in the angry sky, in the troubled water, in the flickering lights. There is some solemn echo of them even in the Cathedral chime, which strikes a sudden surprise to his heart as he turns in under the archway of the gatehouse.

"And so *he* goes up the postern stair."

In these and other such paragraphs, according to Mr Proctor and Mr Lang, Dickens tries to make us think that Edwin is dead: but "any one who understands Dickens's manner" sees through his artifice, and recognises that Edwin, not merely is not marked for death, but is positively designated for life. So far Mr Proctor and Mr Lang appear to be in agreement: but I gather that Mr Proctor justifies his incredulity about Edwin's death principally on the ground that "all the characters who die in Dickens's stories are marked for death from the beginning," and "there is not one note of death in aught that Drood does or says," and only secondarily, by an appeal to the cultivated tact of the expert Dickensian; while Mr Lang, although in passing he endorses Mr Proctor's argument that Dickens' notes or marks of death are conspicuously absent in Drood, relies chiefly upon a general impression which he admits to be "merely subjective." This being so, it will be convenient to separate the two proofs, and to hold Mr Proctor responsible for the one, Mr Lang for the other. Now the fact is that Mr Proctor's argument is ineffective, because he does not tell us what the notes are which from the beginning mark for death the characters who die in Dickens' stories, and in consequence we are not in a position either to consider the validity of the tests or to apply them: and that Mr Lang's argument hardly claims to be a proof. Thus neither appeals to any one who is not already convinced. At the same time I value exceedingly Mr Lang's "subjective impression." He is far more familiar with Dickens' methods, mannerisms, and "tones" than I am : and when he writes—"you can tell, as it were by the sound of the voice of Dickens, that Edwin is to live," I hesitate to set up my own "subjective impression" against his. Nevertheless, if I am asked what subjective impression the paragraphs quoted above and other such produce upon me, I am bound to say that in my judgment they are ominous and tragical, and have the ring of truth. Indeed the impression is so strong with me that, if I were afterwards to find Edwin reappearing alive and well, I should have a resentful feeling that my pity for Drood and my admiration of Dickens had been won by false pretences. But, as I have said, I must not set my subjective impression against the subjective impressions of experts.

There are however other tests to which the theory of Mr Proctor and Mr Lang should be submitted : (1) is the theory that Edwin escaped and reappeared as Datchery plausible in itself? (2) does it harmonise with what we know and conjecture about the tenour of the story?

(1) Mr Proctor and Mr Lang have discussed at length the manner of Edwin's escape. They suppose that "Jasper bungled the murder: made an incomplete job of it," *Puzzle*, p. 57 : either "Drood's face was fortunately protected by the strong silk shawl with which Jasper had intended to throttle him," *Watched*

by the Dead, p. 74, and Durdles by his "gift" happened to discover him in Mrs Sapsea's tomb ; or Jasper, after his night in the opium-den, has one of his weird seizures and "not only fails to strangle Drood, but fails to lock the door of the vault, and Drood walks out after Jasper has gone," *Puzzle*, p. 58.   Having thus escaped, Drood enters into communication with Grewgious and restores the betrothal ring, *Watched by the Dead*, p. 133, and Grewgious, *Watched by the Dead*, p. 83, tells Rosa that Edwin is alive.   He was however, thinks Mr Proctor, who is sometimes very bold, "for months prostrated by illness following Jasper's desperate attack," *Watched by the Dead*, p. 95, and, apparently, when he recovered, he was a changed man, capable of sustaining the arduous part of Datchery.

Now it is, I suppose, conceivable that Jasper, having studiously planned and rehearsed the murder, nevertheless failed in the execution: but, though this is conceivable, I cannot think it probable that what was so carefully planned and rehearsed, would fail so pitiably. By admission, Jasper proposed to strangle Edwin and to bury him in a heap of quicklime.   It is suggested that, in fact, Jasper half strangled him, and buried him in quicklime so imperfectly that a rescue or escape was possible.   This does not seem to me sufficiently plausible.   Mr Lang himself thinks Mr Proctor's theory "thin, very thin," and pronounces his detailed conjectures "crude to the last degree," *Puzzle*, pp. 55, 56.   So far I agree with Mr Lang: but I do not think that Mr Lang's supplementary conjecture— " that Jasper had one of his 'filmy' seizures, was 'in a

frightful sort of dream,' and bungled the murder,"
p. 57—does much to mend matters. If Jasper, in
spite of his seizure, was still able to half strangle Drood,
ransack his pockets, and half bury him in quicklime, it
is difficult to understand how Drood escaped so easily.
If Drood was able with or without help to make his
escape, it is difficult to understand how Jasper succeeded so far as to half strangle him, ransack his
pockets, and half bury him in quicklime.

(2) But in spite of these difficulties let us suppose
that Drood escaped. Our second question remains:
is the theory of Mr Proctor and Mr Lang consistent
with the recorded facts of the rest of the extant fragment? Mr Proctor and Mr Lang assume that
Grewgious, as soon as he arrived at Cloisterham,
became aware of Drood's escape, told Rosa of it, and
received from Drood the betrothal ring. Is this consistent with what we know? If Grewgious is aware
that Drood in the company of Jasper has narrowly
escaped assassination, why does Grewgious allow
Landless to remain under suspicion, and why is
Grewgious' attitude six months later defensive and
not offensive? If the ring has been restored to him,
why does he not make trial of its "invincible force
to hold and drag"? If Rosa knew what Grewgious
is supposed to have known and to have told to her,
Puzzle, p. 62, namely, that Edwin is still alive, would
not this knowledge have coloured her thoughts about
Edwin's disappearance and about the scene in the
garden? and, if it had coloured her thoughts, would
Dickens, who gives us in the third and fourth para-

graphs of ch. xx a careful account of Rosa's speculations
and questionings during the last six months and after
the garden scene, have thought himself justified in
suppressing this principal factor? Again, when Rosa
says, p. 236, "I had no time, I took a sudden resolution.
Poor, poor Eddy!" and Grewgious replies, "Ah, poor
fellow, poor fellow!" they seem to me to recognise
Drood's death[1]: compare *Bleak House*, ch. xlv, p. 574.
I am aware that Mr Proctor, *Watched by the Dead*,
p. 104, interprets otherwise: "'Poor, poor Eddy!' from
her meant that her sudden resolution had no relation
to Edwin's love; and 'Ah, poor fellow, poor fellow!'
from Mr Grewgious was the natural answer to what
her sorrowful words implied": but I confess that this
interpretation seems to me far-fetched.

But besides these particular reasons for believing
that Edwin Drood did not escape, I have further a
general conviction that the story is a better one if it
has for its central incident the extinction of a bright
but careless youth at the moment when he seems to
be awakening to a more purposeful existence, than if
the villain bungles the crime, and is condemned to
death for a consequential homicide.   In my judgment,
if Drood is done to death by his uncle on the fateful
Christmas Eve, we have a real tragedy, and there is
enough for Dickens to do in tracing the steps by which
Grewgious, Datchery, and the opium-woman—not
without help from Durdles and Deputy—brought home

---

[1] Of course at p. 248 the words "Poor, poor Eddy!" thought,
but not spoken, by Rosa, have an entirely different meaning: at
p. 236 she has not yet made acquaintance with Tartar.

to Jasper his criminality.   On the other hand, if Drood
has escaped, I think him a common-place and lucky
young man, and Jasper a common-place and clumsy
scoundrel, and I lose my interest in both.   In a word,
I am bold enough to fancy that the drama which,
according to Mr Proctor, Dickens suggested to his
less instructed readers, would have produced a more
effective dénoûment than the surprise which, according
to the experts, he was preparing for us.   But I frankly
admit that this is equivalent to saying that I am one
of those whom Mr Proctor, *Watched by the Dead,*
p. 145, describes as "the duller readers."

   In conclusion, something must be said about an
objection which at this point may very fairly be raised
against me.   Throughout this section I have assumed
that the "mystery" was a real mystery ; that Jasper
was a veritable criminal who knew what he wanted and
did his best to bring it about ; and, in a word, that the
actions both of Jasper and of the rest were dictated by
common sense.   But are these assumptions justifiable ?
In *Bleak House,* it may be said, where also there is a
mystery, the conduct of the persons concerned is wholly
irrational.   Tulkinghorn is a machiavellian intriguer,
but his aims are wholly unintelligible.   Lady Dedlock
is a bundle of inconsistencies.   Hortense's appearance
at Tulkinghorn's chambers is futile.   Bucket's expedition to St Alban's to make Jo "move on" is silly.
Hortense's murder of Tulkinghorn is as absurd as her
conduct before and afterwards.   Bucket's journey with
Esther Summerson is fantastic.   If in *Bleak House*
Dickens was content to propound a mystery which no

more hangs together than a nightmare, it may fairly be asked by what right I look for consistency in *The Mystery of Edwin Drood*. I look for it, because a careful examination of the extant chapters satisfies me that, here at any rate, Dickens had taken pains in constructing his story. If, as I think, the chronology of the extant chapters is impeccable, I need not expect in the sequel the inconsistencies and the absurdities of *Bleak House*. In the interval Dickens had learnt that a story ought to be plausible and consistent, and I assume that *Edwin Drood* was more or less so.

§ ix. *The manuscript.*

The preceding pages had been written and again and again revised, when I learnt from Dr M. R. James, on the authority of Mr Anstey Guthrie, that the manuscript of the extant chapters of *Edwin Drood* still exists and is preserved at the Victoria and Albert Museum. I have now examined it, and it seems to me worth while to give some account of it, and to consider what light, if any, it throws upon my inquiry.

The volume (Forster Collection No. 167) begins with a page of tentative suggestions for the title of the book and for the names of its personages. Next comes a table of contents for No. VI. The rejected chapter, which Forster prints in the *Life*, follows. Then, headed "Plans," there is a scheme of chapters numbered from I to XX, XX being the end of Number V. Pages are left blank for each of the remaining Numbers. Next we have "Mystery of Edwin Drood. Chapter Headings." The "Chapter Headings" of Parts I to V are numbered from Chapter I (here called "The Dawn") to Chapter XX (here called "Divers Flights"): but these "Headings" were not, I think, filled in here till the chapters had been actually written, and, as I shall presently show, certain of the chapters were subsequently transposed. Then comes the text of the extant chapters, the beginning of each " Number " being indicated, and, in all instances but one, the pages of each Number being numbered consecutively by Dickens himself.

The first section of the manuscript text includes " No. I.   Chapter I, The Prologue," pp. (1) and 2.
> "Chapter II, A Dean and a Chapter also," pp. 3—10.
> " Chapter III, The Nuns' House," pp. 11—17.
> " Chapter IV, Mr Sapsea," pp. 18—23.

And here I may note that at the end of Chapter IV the manuscript has a last rejoinder from Durdles to Jasper which does not appear in the printed text, and that the printed text adds a final paragraph about Jasper and Sapsea which does not appear in the manuscript. I suspect that these changes were made in the proof, and that Dickens sacrificed Durdles' "sulky retort[1]" in order to make room within the limits of the page for the addition of the concluding paragraph.

But, besides these four chapters contained in the first section or " Number " of the manuscript, the printed Part I includes also "chapter v, Mr Durdles and Friend," which in the manuscript appears as

---

[1] Printed text: "and he gets out of the room, deigning no word of answer." Manuscript: "and finally he gets out of the room with the sulky retort: ' How does the fact stand, Mr Jasper? The fact stands six on one side to half a dozen on t'other. So far as Durdles sees the fact with *his* eyes, it has took up about that position as near as may be.' "

"Chapter VIII," pp. 19—23, at the end of the second section. Thus, whereas in the printed book Jasper makes acquaintance with Deputy on the night of the visit to Sapsea, in the manuscript they encounter one another for the first time on the night of Mrs Crisparkle's dinner party, when Jasper returns to the gatehouse after the conversation with Crisparkle recorded at the end of the chapter entitled " Daggers Drawn." Now there can be no doubt that for the general purposes of the story " Mr Durdles and Friend" is better placed after " Mr Sapsea." But transposition, however excellent the motive, has its risks: and the opening words and the closing sentences of "Mr Durdles and Friend," while they are quite appropriate in their original position, are not altogether in keeping where they now stand. For, first, whilst Jasper when he returned to the gatehouse from Crisparkle's house in Minor Canon Corner would necessarily make "his way home through the Close," p. 52, when he returned from Sapsea's he would naturally follow High Street: and, secondly, the careful description of Jasper "looking down upon his nephew with a fixed and deep attention" as he "lies asleep, calm and untroubled," and then "lighting his pipe, and delivering himself to the Spectres it invokes at midnight," whilst it was full of meaning after the scene in "Daggers Drawn," has no special significance as it now stands, and indeed, inasmuch as not one word has been said about Edwin Drood's presence at Cloisterham, is almost, though not quite, an inconsistency.

The second section of the manuscript includes four chapters:

"No. II.   Chapter V, Philanthropy in Minor Canon
          Corner," pp. 1—7, our ch. vi.
          "Chapter VI, More Confidences than One,"
          pp. 7—12, our ch. vii.
          "Chapter VII, Daggers Drawn," pp. 13—18,
          our ch. viii.
          "Chapter VIII, Mr Durdles and Friend,"
          pp. 19—23, our ch. v.

Of these, Chapter VIII has been already appended
as chapter v to Part I of the printed book: and, to
fill the gap thus made in the second Part, Chapter IX
is introduced here from the third section of the
manuscript.

The next instalment of the manuscript includes
four chapters, namely,

"No. III.   Chapter IX, Birds in the Bush," ten pages,
           not numbered by Dickens. As we have
           seen, this chapter was printed in Part II.
"No. III.   Chapter X," but originally "Chapter IX,"
           "Smoothing the Way," pp. (1)—9.
           "Chapter XI, A Picture and a Ring," pp.
           11—18. Page 10, including the first five
           paragraphs of the chapter, is missing:
           but the title is certified by the list of
           "Chapter Headings."
           "Chapter XII, A Night with Durdles," pp.
           19—27.

Now Dickens' procedure is strictly methodical: he

writes at the beginning of the first chapter of the first Number, No. I, and he numbers the pages of the Number consecutively, (1)—23 : and so elsewhere. Here, our "chapter x, Smoothing the Way," was originally "Chapter IX," and the pages of this chapter and the two chapters which followed it are numbered (1)—27. But, as I have said, Dickens has not numbered the pages of "Chapter IX, Birds in the Bush." Whence it appears that when he went to work upon Part III, he began by writing what we know as chapter x, and that he probably wrote Chapter XI and Chapter XII before he wrote Chapter IX. Thus once more Dickens in the printed book departs from what I may call "the order of composition."

So far we are able to compare the manuscript with Parts which Dickens himself prepared for publication and saw published. The three remaining parts appeared after his death.

The fourth section of the manuscript is Part IV of the printed story. It contains

"No. IV. Chapter XIII, Both at their Best," pp. (1)—7.

"Chapter XIV, When shall these three meet again ?" pp. (8)—16.

"Chapter XV, Impeached," pp. (17)—22.

"Chapter XVI, Devoted," pp. (22)—27.

The next section of the manuscript, the fifth, consists of four chapters, entitled respectively

"No. V. Chapter XVII, Philanthropy, Professional and Unprofessional," pp. 1—9.

       "Chapter XVIII, A settler in Cloisterham,"
       pp. 10—14.
       "Chapter XIX, Shadow on the Sundial,"
       pp. 15—18.
       "Chapter XX, Divers Flights," pp. 19—27.

But (1) what is here described as "Chapter XVIII" was originally "Chapter XIX," and the pages 10, 11, with which it opens, were originally pages 14, 15 : and what is here described as "Chapter XIX" was originally "Chapter XVIII," and its pages 15, 16, 17, 18, were originally pages 10, 11, 12, 13. That is to say, Dickens wrote the whole of "Chapter XIX, Shadow on the Sundial," before he wrote the earlier half of "Chapter XVIII, A Settler in Cloisterham," and presumably decided to transpose the two chapters before he wrote the latter half of Chapter XVIII. Furthermore, (2) "Chapter XX, Divers Flights," includes the two chapters called in the printed book "chapter xx, A Flight," and "chapter xxi, A Recognition." Obviously, when the manuscript was set up by the printers, Forster found that there was more matter than was wanted to fill the customary thirty-two pages. So he divided the chapter called "Divers Flights" into two chapters, and reserved the second, "A Recognition," for the sixth Part. He would be well pleased to do this, because in this way he would bring the sixth and last Part to very nearly the customary tale of pages. Moreover, he may have felt as I do, some doubt about Dickens' meaning in describing Chapter XX by the title "Divers Flights": for it is not clear what "Flight" other than Rosa's is here referred to. A note in " Plans,"—" Edwin disappears : *done already*"—suggests that Dickens was thinking of Edwin's disappearance six months before, and that he should have written "Another Flight."

However this may be, the sixth section of the manuscript consists of " No. VI, Chapter XXI, A Gritty State of Things comes on," pp. (1)—10, that is to say, our chapter xxii, and " Chapter XXII, The Dawn Again," pp. 11—20, that is to say, our chapter xxiii. Dickens had intended to add to the Number a " Chapter XXIII": but there is nothing to show what was to be included in it. Thus in the printed text, the sixth Part contains " chapter xxi, A Recognition," " chapter xxii, A Gritty State of Things comes on," " chapter xxiii, The Dawn again."

Such are the facts about the manuscript. It may be worth while to recapitulate them in a tabular form.

N.B. (1) ch. v of the book was written after chapters vi, vii, viii: (2) ch. ix was written after ch. x was begun: (3) ch. xix was written before ch. xviii; but before C. D. had completed ch. xviii, he resolved to transpose the two chapters: (4) Ch. XX of the MS was divided, presumably by Forster, into ch. xx and ch. xxi of the book, because C. D. had left too much "copy' for Part v, and too little for Part vi.

It remains for me to consider whether the evidence of the manuscript adds to, or detracts from, such results as I had previously obtained: and, in particular, whether it encourages or discourages my theory that "xviii, A Settler in Cloisterham" appears prematurely in the printed text.

My contention is that, whoever Datchery may be, his settlement at Cloisterham is intelligible so soon as the Staple Inn allies have cognisance of Rosa's interview with Jasper, and no sooner. Now the manuscript shows that Dickens had described that interview before Datchery appears on the scene. But though Jasper has said to Rosa what should rouse the allies from their apathy and cause them to set a watch at Cloisterham, his threats cannot produce this effect until they are reported at Staple Inn : and therefore, except as another proof that Dickens sometimes altered the order of his chapters, the fact that "Shadow on the Sundial" originally preceded "A Settler at Cloisterham" in no wise helps my argument. Indeed it tells against it; inasmuch as Dickens has made an alteration, and the alteration which he has made is not that which I desiderate.

We have however, within the limits of the three Parts printed in Dickens' lifetime, decisive evidence that neither the order of composition nor the order of the manuscript nor the agreement of the order of composition and the order of the manuscript proves the order of events and the order of publication. For, first, the continuous paging of No. II v, vi, vii, viii, shows that viii was written after v, vi, vii: yet Dickens ultimately placed viii at the end of Part I as chapter v. And, secondly, while the numeral III shows that the chapter entitled " Birds in the Bush," which was not paged by Dickens, was intended for the third Number, the continuous paging of "Smoothing the Way" and the two following chapters from 1 to 27 shows that X, XI, XII were written before the unpaged IX, and the numerals III IX, originally prefixed to " Smoothing the Way " point in the same direction. Thus here too the order of publication is different from the order of composition : but in this instance Dickens has altered the numeration, and accordingly the order in the bound volume of manuscript agrees with the order of publication.

This being so, when I suppose that Dickens, if he had lived, would have placed xviii between xxii and xxiii, my hypothesis is neither illegitimate nor far-fetched. As I have said, I am led to it by what I understand to be the requirements of the situation, and I regard Dickens' fear, expressed to his sister-in-law, that he had introduced Datchery too soon[1], as a strong confirmation of my conjecture. Moreover, Dickens might easily be tempted to embark prematurely upon this part of his story. The introduction of the watcher

[1] "The explanation of it " [the rejected fragment] "perhaps is, that, having become a little nervous about the course of the tale, from a fear that he might have plunged too soon into the incidents leading on to the catastrophe, such as the Datchery assumption in the fifth number (a misgiving he had certainly expressed to his sister-in-law), it had occurred to him to open some fresh veins of character incidental to the interest, though not directly part of it." *Life*, iii, 432. See above, pp. 36, 37.

with his notable personality must have interested
Dickens intensely. Indeed, as we know, he had
already experimented in the conversation between
Sapsea and Poker, *Life*, iii, 438. The vague phrase
with which xviii begins—"At about this time"—looks
as if it had been deliberately chosen with a view to the
subsequent placing of a chapter written in advance.
In a word, it is certain that in *Edwin Drood* the order
of composition is not necessarily the order of events or
the order of publication : but the manuscript affords no
evidence that Dickens intended to place "A Settler at
Cloisterham" next before "The Dawn Again."

Furthermore, in the section called "Plans" there are
one or two hints which are worth recording. Thus upon
"Smoothing the Way" Dickens notes—"That is, for
Jasper's plan, through Mr Crisparkle, who takes new
ground on Neville's new confidence." That is to say,
when Crisparkle, on the strength of his conversation
with Neville, goes to Jasper to ask his help in
"smoothing the way" to a reconciliation between the
two young fellows, he is unconsciously "smoothing the
way" for Jasper's revised scheme. Again, "Plans" has a
concise but fairly complete summary of "xvi, Devoted":
"Jasper's artful use of the communication on his re-
covery. Cloisterham Weir, Mr Crisparkle, and the
watch and pin. Jasper's artful turn. The DEAN.
Neville cast out. Jasper's diary. 'I devote myself
to his destruction.'" That is to say, Jasper, as soon
as he recovers from the shock of Grewgious' news,
"artfully" counterfeits hope and candour ; and when
Crisparkle has found the watch and the pin at the

Weir, "artfully" alleges this discovery as a new ground for suspecting and pursuing Neville. Now these notes, and in particular the notes on xvi, dispose of a doubt which I had once entertained about Dickens' conception of Jasper's character. In ch. iii, p. 30, Dickens echoes a theory of the operation of opium which is propounded by Wilkie Collins in the *Moonstone*—"as, in some cases of drunkenness, and in others of animal magnetism, there are two states of consciousness which never clash, but each of which pursues its separate course as though it were continuous instead of broken (thus, if I hide my watch when I am drunk, I must be drunk again before I can remember where), so Miss Twinkleton has two distinct and separate phases of being." Observing this, I had wondered whether Dickens supposed Jasper, though he had planned the murder in his waking moments, to have executed it when he was under the influence of opium, and when he awoke to have no memory of what he had done. The notes which I have quoted from "Plans" satisfy me that there is no ground whatever for any such supposition : Dickens sees in Jasper an example of "the criminal intellect, which its own professed students perpetually misread, because they persist in trying to reconcile it with the average intellect of average men, instead of identifying it as a horrible wonder apart," p. 233; and accordingly, at p. 253, Grewgious describes him as "a brigand and a wild beast in combination." Dickens has not, then, as I had once feared, complicated his story by imagining his villain to be a dual personality, sometimes plotting a crime, sometimes shrinking from it in horror : he makes him an unmitigated scoundrel, ruthless, remorseless, and, withal, resourceful, so that, even when he learns that the murder of Edwin has been futile, he immediately perceives that the story of the broken engagement may divert suspicion from Neville, and proceeds to devise a new way of directing suspicion towards him.

And now I must call attention to a fact which may seem to favour the theory of Mr Proctor and Mr Lang. I have mentioned that the manuscript volume begins with a page of tentative suggestions for the title of the book and for the names of its personages. The experimental titles are " The loss of James (Edwyn) Wakefield," " James's Disappearance," " Flight and Pursuit," " Sworn to avenge it," " One object in Life," "A Kinsman's Devotion," "The Two Kinsmen," "The loss of Edwin Brude," " The Mystery in the Drood Family," " The loss of Edwyn Drood," " The flight of Edwin Drood," " Edwin Drood in hiding," " The loss of Edwin Drude," " The Disappearance of Edwin Drood," "The Mystery of Edwin Drood," "Dead? or Alive?" Two of these titles, " The flight of Edwin Drood" and "Edwin Drood in hiding," may be thought to suggest that Drood escaped: but, inasmuch as Dickens plainly means to leave it doubtful to the last, I can hardly think that they are decisive[1].

[1] I may here comment upon two or three textual errors which have attracted my attention. (1) The opening sentences of the story are: "An ancient English Cathedral Tower? How can the ancient English Cathedral tower be here! The well-known massive gray square tower of its old Cathedral? How can that be here!"

The possessive pronoun "its" has no meaning. Plainly, in the second sentence, "town" should be substituted for "tower": "How can the ancient English Cathedral town be here!" So the MS. (2) In ch. xix "Shadow on the Sundial," p. 225, Jasper, appealing to Rosa, speaks of Edwin Drood's portrait of her, "which I feigned to hang always in my sight for his sake, but worshipped in torment for years." Instead of "for *years*," read "for *yours*," that is to say "for your sake," in opposition to "for his sake." The manuscript gives this reading, and it is obviously right: for, plainly, Jasper had not been long resident at Cloisterham. (3) In the last chapter, p. 285, the printed texts have, "Its antiquities and ruins are surpassingly beautiful, with a lusty ivy gleaming in the sun, and the rich trees waving in the balmy air." For "a lusty ivy," read, with the manuscript, "the lusty ivy." (4) In ch. xvi, p. 197, Dickens calls "Minor Canon *Corner*" by its real name, "Minor Canon *Row*," just as in *Lothair* Disraeli for once forgot himself, and called a· contemporary ecclesiastic, not Catesby, but, by his real name, Capell.

In the "Plans," the Landlesses were named, with a query, Neville and Olympia Heyridge or Heyfort: and the Verger, whom we know as Tope, was called Peptune.

§ x. *Conclusion.*

Let me now formulate the principal issues, and state summarily the views which have been taken about them.

(1) *Did Jasper attempt to murder Drood?* Mr Proctor, Mr Cuming Walters, Mr Lang, and, so far as I know, all who have handled the subject, hold, as I do, that Jasper attempted to murder Drood.

(2) *What was the scene of the attempted murder?* According to Mr Cuming Walters, and, apparently, according to Mr Proctor, the scene of the attempted murder was "near the Cathedral," *Clues*, p. 33, —that is to say, outside it. Mr Lang, *Puzzle*, p. 56, thinks that Jasper, having led Drood into the Sapsea vault in the graveyard, imperfectly strangled him there. According to Mr Charles, Jasper strangled Drood at the gatehouse. According to Mr G. F. Gadd (*Dickensian*, iv, 102), Jasper, having strangled Drood "on the top of the tower," "topples the body over into that 'stillest part' where the tomb awaits it." Mr H. Hall (*Dickensian*, i, 250) makes "the great tower of the Cathedral the scene of the tragedy." In my opinion, Jasper bonneted Drood with the scarf as

they descended the staircase of the Cathedral tower, and flung him down the steep steps.

(3) *Where did Jasper deposit Edwin's body?* The body was deposited, according to Mr Lang and Mr Charles in the Sapsea tomb in the graveyard; according to Mr Proctor and Mr Cuming Walters in a (supposed) Sapsea vault in the crypt. My own conviction is that Jasper buried it in a heap of lime in the crypt of the Cathedral.

(4) *Did Drood escape, and, if so, how?* Mr Proctor thought that Durdles found Drood buried in quick-lime: but "his face was fortunately protected" by Jasper's scarf, and Durdles and Deputy carried him to the Travellers' Lodgings, where Grewgious joined them. Mr Lang conjectures that Jasper "had one of his 'filmy' seizures," "bungled the murder," and "failed to lock the door of the vault," and that "Edwin opened the door, and walked out," *Puzzle*, pp. 58, 59. Mr Cuming Walters and Mr Charles think that Drood did *not* escape, and I agree with them.

(5) *Who is Datchery?* According to Mr Proctor and Mr Lang, Datchery is Edwin Drood. According to Mr Charles and others, Datchery is Bazzard, but a Bazzard transformed out of all recognition, a Bazzard who does not "follow" but leads. According to Mr G. F. Gadd, *Dickensian*, ii, 12 ff., Datchery is Tartar. According to my friend "F. C. B.," *Cambridge Review*, 1906, p. 185, Datchery is Neville Landless. According to a writer in the *Cornhill Magazine* for March 1884, Datchery is a clever de-

tective.   According to Mr Cuming Walters, Datchery
is Helena Landless.   For myself, I dismiss the identi-
fications of Datchery, who interests me profoundly,
with Drood, Bazzard, Tartar, and Neville Landless,
as wholly impossible : I regard the theory of the
anonymous writer in the *Cornhill* as possible, but im-
probable : and I think, with Mr Cuming Walters, that
Helena Landless, who first proposed to set a watch
upon Jasper, was herself the watcher.

And now I will put a question which, so far as I
know, has not been raised by any one, and, I must
confess, seems to me insoluble.   The last words of the
first chapter are : "and then the intoned words, 'WHEN
THE WICKED MAN—' rise among groins of arches and
beams of roof, awakening muttered thunder": and in
the part of the manuscript which is headed "Plans"
one of the supplementary notes for this chapter is
"Touch the key note—'when the wicked man.'"   I
ask then, (6) *is Dickens thinking of these four words
only, or has he in his mind the whole text?*   In other
words, does he wish to suggest to us that Jasper is
"a wicked man," or are we to expect his repent-
ance at the end of the story?   I have no answer to
propose.

Printed in the United States
By Bookmasters